ELECTION 97

Election '97

A CHRISTIAN VIEW OF THE MAJOR ISSUES

Christopher Graffius

Hodder & Stoughton
LONDON SYDNEY AUCKLAND

British Library Cataloguing in Publication Data
A record for this book is available from the British Library

ISBN 0 340 64165 7

Typeset by Hewer Text Composition Services, Edinburgh
Printed and bound in Great Britain by
Cox & Wyman Ltd, Reading, Berks.

Hodder and Stoughton Ltd
A Division of Hodder Headline PLC
338 Euston Road
London NW1 3BH

Contents

Introduction

Democracy thrives on information, and information is power. A general election is the ultimate exercise of the people's power to sit in judgment on their political representatives and it is therefore important that electors have as much information as possible on those who solicit their votes. Getting that information to the voters during a general election is part of the mission of the Movement for Christian Democracy, for whom I act as General Secretary, and this book sets out to review the political battle and provide some of the information.

Politics, particularly the confrontational variety we practise in Britain, begs one to take sides. I have tried to resist that temptation and to tell it as it is, attempting to give each party a fair crack of the whip when describing their positions, and where space and information allow also to present some of the criticisms of that position. I do not claim to have been successful all the time and I'm sure that my personal views will have crept into my text. I do not apologise for that, and hope that taking a robust position will make the book more interesting than the dreary recital of policy statements that we are usually treated to in the manifestos. I do apologise if I have unwittingly misrepresented any of the politicians or parties, but I would add that political parties are more than a little coy about giving out information on their positions. I will not trouble you with the details except to say that getting policy statements out of the parties is rather like wringing water from rocks, impossible at the best of times and unlikely to yield useful results. There is one exception to this, and that is the Liberal Democrats who at first glance appear to have a policy on everything and are only too willing to shower you with the papers describing it. There may be reasons for this. The Liberal Democrats have one of the most detailed and democratic policy-making procedures in politics; they also suffer from a lack of press coverage, and publishing policy statements is a good way of securing column inches as well as informing those are interested in the general population.

I would also like to make clear that this book is not a guide to Movement for Christian Democracy policy. There are occasions when I have described MCD policy and I have always attributed it. Other than this any of the views expressed are my own and are made in a personal capacity. I would be delighted to send readers further details of MCD thinking if they wish. Nor is this book solely for Christians. We live in a society where up to 60 per cent of people believe in a God but where only 10 per cent of people go to church. Many more than that 60 per cent give some support to Christian values and ethics and this book is as much for the general reader as for Christians.

Some politicians have taken exception to Christians making political statements from their own standpoint. The same politicians have often criticised the Church for a lack of involvement in society, which they say contributes to social dislocation and moral collapse. They cannot have it both ways. Christians have as much right as any other group in society to fight their corner within our democratic system.

Election guides tend to concentrate on electoral figures and ignore the policy battle. This guide seeks to provide an easily accessible review of party policy so that the reader can discover where each party stands and then weigh the importance of particular policies when determining their vote. The only definitive guides to policy produced for an election are the party manifestos, but they are of little help. These documents, normally published less than a month before polling day, are designed to put across an attractive message while causing the least possible offence. Ambiguities and half-explanations are included to give the party room for manoeuvre if it should be elected. Despite this, manifestos can often be seen as a binding contract with the voters. In one famous case it was the position of a comma in a previous manifesto that stopped Mrs Thatcher taxing child benefit.

The first part of this book concentrates on the story of Christian involvement in politics and considers its justification. It reviews the various expressions of Christian politics and sets out some of the common principles of Christian social thought. This should provide benchmarks by which to assess the policies described in the second part. For those who wish to pursue the matter further, the third section describes how you can become involved in an election campaign by lobbying the candidates, holding election meetings and days of prayer and working on a candidate's campaign.

A word of warning. Political parties announce new policy positions or define earlier announcements right down to the wire on election day. Announcing new initiatives gets publicity and every party regards publicity much as a normal person regards oxygen. The accounts of policy in this book should be read in the light of any subsequent announcements following publication.

Elections are crucially important for the future of the country and involve a considerable amount of hard work, but they are also great fun. My first political involvement took the form of assisting a candidate in a rural Scottish constituency in 1983. I caught the bug immediately and have been involved in every election, and quite a few by-elections in between. I hope that you find the process of democracy and the battle of ideas as fascinating as I do.

Christopher Graffius

A Christian Political Perspective

Christian involvement in British politics

To our ancestors the notion that religion was separate from politics would have seemed both subversive and bizarre. As believers themselves they thought that all power comes from God and that churchmen and politicians would be ultimately accountable before the highest throne of all. It was not that they equated religion with politics – they distinguished between the spiritual authority of the Church and the temporal power of the secular state – but they believed that both powers were ultimately striving towards the same goal: a Christian nation. Dissent or unbelief were seen as threats to the security of the state, because they struck at the spiritual roots of the nation and our ancestors cared so deeply for this that they were prepared to martyr each other to preserve their version of the truth. In the English Civil War both sides claimed religious truth for themselves. Cavaliers went to war in support of the Divine Right of Kings, Roundheads for the purity of the Protestant faith. All this left Cromwell to muse: 'Each man who wages war believes that God is on his side. I'll wager God must wonder who is on his.'

It was the Enlightenment and rationalism that first threatened the notion of a Christian basis to politics. The cultured and sceptical oligarchs who ruled eighteenth-century Britain marginalised and privatised their faith. A politician in the age of Fox or Wilkes was rated by his performance at the gaming tables of the London clubs, his mistresses and the wealth of his patrons. It was into this scene that William Wilberforce stepped, as a young man of fashion admired for his success in the drawing-rooms of the rich rather than his performance in Parliament. But it is an effect of faith that when Christ changes us we change the lives of others and Wilberforce went through a conversion experience that not only changed his life but had a far-reaching impact on the political nation.

Wilberforce's first instinct was to abandon Parliament, 'that stage for prizefighters' as he called it. His new Christian friends protested, and Wilberforce remained to form the 'Clapham Sect' and launch his two great campaigns to end slavery and 'reform the manners and morals of the nation'. Wilberforce is now more remembered for the fight against slavery, but as a human rights campaigner he foreshadowed many of the tactics of our own time. He formed networks to support the campaign in the country, and newspapers were used and briefing notes produced to inform and co-ordinate the campaign. In Parliament Wilberforce and his colleagues fought a slow war of attrition with those who represented the vested interests of the slave owners and traders, and who justified the horrors of the slave trade by recourse to economics or even the Bible. As he lay on his deathbed Wilberforce was brought the news that his Bill to abolish slavery within the British Empire had been passed. Shortly afterwards he was visited by a young Tory MP whose family had made its fortune from slavery and who had voted against abolition. That meeting with Wilberforce so influenced the young man that he left a changed man. His name was Gladstone, and he went on to become the 'grand old man' of Victorian politics, three times Prime Minister and a politician who was always prepared to put his faith before his party.

It was Wilberforce's second campaign that left the greatest legacy for his country. He had always argued that religion was a necessary basis for any society and that Christianity was the best religion for a secure state. Tackling the corruption of Georgian England he encouraged the political classes to rediscover their faith and their responsibility for the faith of those they ruled. Setting an example of regular church-going and prayer for the tenants or forming societies of middle-class ladies for the relief of the urban poor may now seem archaic, but in their own time these began a revival of faith that worked out in society in the form of a new ethic of public service. It was that concept which, refined and strengthened by the Victorians, has lasted down to our own times.

It has been fashionable to ridicule the values and faith of Victorian Britain. Academics have made careers in pointing out much of the closet hypocrisy, colonial exploitation and poverty that marked the nineteenth century. To concentrate on this is to tell only part of the story. It ignores the expansion in education, much of it free to the poor. It ignores the emphasis on values of community, thrift, the family and neighbourliness that made Victorian Britain a remarkably secure society. It also ignores the explosion of private, voluntary, charitable associations working at every level and in every part of society to relieve poverty and care for those for whom the state did not provide. In our own time this culture of voluntaryism has been lost as the state took over its role, and now most of us hark back to it as a quality which we must rediscover and reinvigorate. Nor would it be right to concentrate on the moralising tendency in much of Victorian puritanism without emphasising the Christian care pioneered by such men as Lord Shaftesbury for children and factory workers, or even Gladstone as Prime Minister scouring the streets to rescue those forced into prostitution.

The Victorian age also saw the birth of our major political parties and because of the close association between faith and politics Christians were influential in their founding. This immediately set Britain apart from continental Europe in her political development. On the continent Europe was plagued by a rash of harshly atheistic and anticlerical governments. Churches were attacked, and the whole way of life of the Christian communities was under threat. As a result Christians came together in denominational parties to defend their rights and privileges and it was these parties that afterwards flowered into modern Christian Democracy. It was a legacy of the central place of faith in British politics that the same thing did not happen here. All parties valued the Christian inspiration at their roots. Conservatives formed strong links with the established Church. We all know that Labour owes more to Methodism than to Marx. The Liberal Party counted for its activists on the Nonconformist Churches while a strong trade unionism grew

from the chapels whose names are still remembered in modern
union terminology.

The nineteenth century also saw the emancipation of Catholics,
barred from political office and activity since the sixteenth century
and harking back to an older tradition of Christian political
activity exemplified by men such as Thomas More, and a widening
franchise due to the Great Reform Acts that passed the vote
down from a propertied elite to all adult males and ultimately,
in the 1920s, to women. The contribution of Christians at this
period to the political health of the nation was wide-ranging
and long-lasting. Liberals can boast the contribution of men like
Lord Acton, a Catholic, who coined the often misquoted phrase
that 'power corrupts, and absolute power corrupts absolutely',
and their Christian contribution has lasted to our own days
with MPs such as David Alton, Simon Hughes and Alan
Beith. Conservatives can look in the last century to men
like Wilberforce and Shaftesbury; in recent times the New
Right contained Christians such as Brian Griffiths, head of
the Downing Street Policy Unit under Mrs Thatcher, whose
own politics owed a considerable amount to her Nonconformist
roots. But there is also a kinder tradition of One Nation Toryism
championed by Christian Conservatives such as Chris Patten,
David Hunt and Patrick Cormack. Labour can look to men
like Kier Hardie, its first MP, who said once that he followed
no other leader than 'the carpenter from Nazareth', and there
may be about to be a renaissance in Christian Socialism. The
influence of Blair's own membership of the Christian Socialist
Movement, and John Smith's commitment to the same cause, has
made membership a popular badge of loyalty to the modernism
within the party, although there still exists a more class-oriented
strain of Christian Socialism epitomised by men like the late Eric
Heffer or the passionate Scottish MP Denis Canavan.

There have been other Christians active in politics throughout
our own century: men like John Wheatley, the Labour minister
who in 1924 introduced council housing in the first Labour
government, and a host of other politicians whose activities
were informed by Christian principles. But from the beginning
of the century there had been a tension in all parties between

those who worked from a Christian inspiration and those who came espousing a new secularism that rejected belief and looked instead to other values. A good example of this struggle is the fight for the soul of the Labour Party between Christian Socialists, exemplified by the thought of Archbishop Temple and R.H. Tawny, and those of a more humanist corporatist strain. The latter group won the struggle. Christian Socialism, which had conceived the Labour Party as also addressing the spiritual side of man, declined to a shadow of its former influence as a Labour Party obsessed with equality and technology took its place.

Christian orthodoxy took a pounding in the 1960s. The governments of both parties developed a liberal, permissive consensus on social reform. Legislation on divorce and abortion provides only two examples of the triumph of secularism at this time. The Christian constituency was caught asleep at its post. Catholics had inherited a tradition of political quietism that went back to the Elizabethan persecutions, Conservative and charismatic evangelical had retreated into a defence of Biblical authority and were just beginning to rediscover the social Gospel. Denominational splits, suspicions and tensions did the rest; there was no concerted Christian opposition to the secular revolution of the sixties. The mood of the times reflected the legislation. 'Morality' became a dirty word in political circles, redolent of authoritarianism and regression. Many Christians in the country gave up on politics, regarding it as a dirty game and considering their vote, if they exercised it, as merely an opportunity to choose the least evil from a range of poor choices. Those Christians who did enter politics were advised to choose a party and attempt to Christianise it from within. They entered a world of privatised faith, where their beliefs, if they were open about them, branded them as marginalised and eccentric. There was little or no cross-party co-operation between Christians. This strategy of benevolent entryism failed the Faith and its failure was measured by the decline in the Christian groups within the parties, which dropped far below the rate that could have been expected given the numbers of Christians within the country. For example, by 1994 the Liberal Democrat Christian Forum had shrunk to 200 members out of a party membership of over

80,000, and these figures and percentages could be duplicated for the other parties.

For those Christians who wished to combine a moral orthodoxy with social commitment, there was no one party which reflected this mix. The right might in general be strong on morality but it was a disaster on social justice. The left might be excellent on social justice but it fell apart on moral orthodoxy. It was these problems that the Movement for Christian Democracy was formed to face.

Christian political theory

It is important to realise that Christianity is not the sole preserve of any political ideology. Nor, for that matter, is Christian political activity going to usher in the Kingdom, but if our faith should inspire every area of our lives then Christian activity in politics is important. It is particularly crucial because politics sets the terms by which people live. It's because of this that Martin Luther King could say that any Christianity that took no account of the slums people live in or the harsh economic and social conditions that affect their lives and relationships is a 'dry as dust religion.' There are those that argue that the fact that you are unemployed, starving and homeless has nothing to do with your spiritual state. I have always found this surprising. If these conditions affect our responses to other people and our relationships with them, then they will also affect our response to God, our relationship with him and our service to him in the people around us. As Bishop Desmond Tutu said: 'Those that say that politics and religion don't mix are not reading the same Bible as me.'

Christians have been present in most forms of political activity and even in places where we would be shocked to find them. We should never forget that Christians played a leading role in the apartheid regime in South Africa, in the system of segregation in the American South and on both sides of the divide in Northern Ireland. We know that they were wrong to attempt to justify discrimination on the grounds of colour or creed from their Bibles, but they would have protested that they were inspired by their faith. It serves as a salutary lesson to us all that an appeal to Christian values by the politician does not confer infallibility and that Christians are just as likely to make a mess of politics as those without any faith.

Currently it is Christian involvement in American politics that receives most coverage in the media. The right-wing, moral-majoritarian views of the Christian Coalition are not typical of Christian involvement in the States, even if they command more airtime. But there is an older and more widespread tradition of Christian political involvement that crosses the denominations and is reflected in most countries within Europe, Latin and South America and increasingly in Africa and South East Asia. Christian Democracy was born in the European denominational parties of the European mainland. It came of age in the recon-struction of Europe after the Second World War. Christian Democrats are just as fallible as any other political group and the number of Italian Christian Democrats accused of corruption has recently begun to approach the numbers of Italian Socialists who have suffered a similar fate. But Christian Democracy has reflected a synthesis of Christian principles that grew out of both the Reformed and Catholic traditions and has been given particular expression by the series of papal social encyclicals produced since the publication of *Rerum Novarum* in 1891.

The first to use the term 'Christian Democracy' were the worker priests at the forefront of the French Revolution before it turned into a retributive bloodbath, and the social justice for all people that they sought has remained an integral part of the Christian Democrat mission. But the denominational parties formed in the nineteenth century came from within what Professor Michael Fogarty has called the Christian *laager* (a defensive ring). They were formed to protect the Faith and to support Christian schooling and other features of their community life which was under threat.

The only grouping to transcend this vision before the Second World War was the Italian Popular or People's Party, formed and led by the fiery Sicilian priest, Don Luigi Sturzo. Sturzo wanted his party to appeal to all, whether they were Christian or not, and for that reason the word 'Christian' did not appear in the party's title. Sturzo had cut his political teeth fighting the great landlords of southern Italy on behalf of a poverty-stricken peasantry, and his party did remarkably well in pre-war elections. Resolutely opposed to Fascism and the rise of Mussolini, the Popular Party became a casualty of the Lateran Treaty between the Vatican and the Blackshirts. To avoid the destruction of the Church the papacy withdrew its encouragement from Sturzo. He died an exile in London during the Second World War.

Other Christian Democrats spent the war years in exile, in hiding or in Fascist concentration camps: Konrad Adenauer was imprisoned by the Gestapo in Germany, de Gasperi spent the war in the Vatican library. There was a general feeling among Christians that they had failed in their resistance to Fascism and that any reconstruction of society after the end of the war depended on a rediscovery of Judaeo-Christian values. Thus Pastor Niemöller could bemoan the fact that he had failed to speak out against the arrests of Jews and trade unionists. Jacques Maritain, the core philosopher of twentieth-century Christian Democracy, in exile in America wrote *Christianity and Democracy* (Geoffrey Bles: London, 1945) during the dark days of 1942, when it was circulated in secret in France. He could look forward to the coming reconstruction with the words:

> It is the task of a supreme effort of human freedom, in the mortal struggle in which it is today engaged, to ensure that the age which we are entering is not the age of the masses and of the shapeless multitudes nourished, brought into subjection and led to the slaughter by infamous demigods, but rather the age of the people and of the man of common humanity – citizen and co-inheritor of the civilised community – cognizant of the dignity of the human person in himself, builder of a more human world directed toward an historic ideal of human brotherhood . . . We do not believe that paradise will be achieved tomorrow; but the task to which we are summoned, the task we have to pursue with all the more courage and hope because at each moment it will be betrayed by human weakness, this task must have for its objective a world of free men imbued in its secular substance by a genuine and living Christianity, a world in

which the inspiration of the Gospel will orientate common
life toward an heroic humanism.

In the aftermath of war Christian Democracy began the task
of reconstruction, and played the leading role not only in the
economic miracles of continental Europe but also in defending
the West against the very real threat of a Stalinist Communist
take-over. In the early years after 1945 Italy very nearly went
the same way as Yugoslavia. That it didn't was a tribute to
the early Christian Democrat governments lead by de Gasperi.
The Christian Democrats put co-operation between nations as a
priority. Europe should never again face the horrors of the wars
that had devastated it in the past. It was no coincidence that
the founding fathers of the European Community, Adenauer,
de Gasperi and Robert Schumann, were Christian Democrats
all, and they passed to the Community much of the Christian
Democrat thought that inspires its ideals to this day.

At the root of this system of thought is a Christian recognition
of the nature and destiny of man. Humanity is created in the image
of God, and this fact, for the Christian, confers on each person a
special value and a unique dignity. Man is the subject, not the
object, of politics and all political endeavour should be directed
at creating a society in which humanity can follow Christ's call
to love God and neighbour. The dignity of man confers rights
balanced by responsibilities. Chief among human rights is the
right to life, without which all other rights cannot be exercised,
but that right also entails a responsibility to respect innocent life
because of its status as a God-given gift.

God created man with the liberty of free will but man was
also created to live in community. This balance of freedom and
responsibilities to others presumes limits on liberty but also
demands a tolerance which is an essential element of a successful
modern pluralist state. Christian Democracy stands at a distance
from the Church and has never been run by clerics. Equally it
has always sought to attract support from non-Christian groups
who nevertheless would approve of its basic values. In this sense
Christian Democracy is a political force for a plural state. The
business of politics is to set the limits on liberty and to assist in

regulating society, where necessary, to ensure the opportunity to respond to Christ's call to all humanity. In this Christian political theory has been guided by several principles including personalism, communitarianism, solidarity and subsidiarity.

Personalism expresses the truth of man's unique creation and his communal responsibilities; it can be defined as a Christian-inspired view of man, striking the balance between the individualism of Liberal Conservatives and the corporatist, statist approach of socialism. Man works out his service to God and neighbour in his relationships and interaction in the communities he participates in, whether at work, home or in church. Christian Democracy has always been keen to empower free people living in their communities and exercising their responsibilities to each other.

This co-operation between people demands a social solidarity and therefore Christian Democrats have never had any time for the politics of class or the politics of envy. True social solidarity means that society's enterprise and work is viewed as in part a corporate effort for the benefit of all rather than a money-grubbing exploitation for the benefit of the few. Christian Democrats are not starry-eyed about the need for leadership, management and the value of property, but these do not absolve the leaders in society from having a care for their workforce and the communities in which they live. Just as the workforce has a right to organise for mutual benefit it must never use its corporate power to destroy the enterprise or demand more than it is due.

The notion of subsidiarity appears first in a papal encyclical against Fascism. It has been misinterpreted by many since it appeared as a guiding European principle within the Maastricht Treaty. The Opposition in Britain has tended to interpret it as meaning devolution pure and simple, that all power should be passed to the lowest level. Conservatives have taken it to mean the independence of the nation state while destroying or centralising the powers previously held by British local government. Its correct interpretation can be summed up in the phrase that power should be allocated as low as possible, but as high as necessary. It is pointless to expect a local authority to tackle national pollution, but equally it is crazy to occupy Parliament's time with matters involving the local collection of rubbish in any particular area. The guiding factors behind subsidiarity are involvement and efficiency, ensuring local involvement among the people that politics affects but ensuring an efficient distribution of powers to create the best political service for all.

All this is summed up in Christian Democracy's objective of the 'common good', a phrase which distinguishes it from the goal of the greatest happiness for the greatest number, the aim of secular utilitarianism, the dominant philosophy in other political movements. The latter in its objective of happiness for the greatest number presumes the exclusion of the minority. The Common Good embraces everyone, whether from the majority or the minority.

Christian Democracy has taken these themes and won widespread support for policies drawn from them. Christian Democrats form the second-largest group – known as the European People's Party – within the European Parliament, securing over thirty million votes. They have played a part in the coalition governments of every European state as either a senior or a junior member of the governing coalition. They have also been prey to all the temptations that power brings; their situation in Italy is an obvious example of this. More insidiously, like every other political party the experience of holding power leads them to face compromises with the secular ideals they oppose. As a result Christian Democracy has been through periods of renewal and is currently engaged in assimilating the Christian Democrat groupings that have sprung up in Eastern Europe, many of them closer to their campaigning Christian enthusiasm than the Western parties.

The Movement for Christian Democracy

In January 1989 a group of twenty-five people met at Prinknash Abbey in Gloucestershire to discuss both the role of Christians in politics and how they could promote Judaeo-Christian values in the political system. The meeting was convened by David Alton MP, the Liberal Democrat member for Liverpool, Mossley Hill, and Ken Hargreaves MP, the Conservative member for Hyndburn. Those who had been invited formed a broad cross-section of Christians working in politics. There were lobbyists, government advisors, researchers, academics and journalists. They came from a wide range of denominations and many of them had been active on David Alton's Bill to limit abortion in the preceding year. That Bill had brought together Christian groups who had not previously co-operated and there was now the question, given the fact that Christian values were widely discounted in an increasingly secular state, of whether Christians could band together to increase the influence of Christian values.

That first weekend ended with the formation of the 'Epiphany Group', which would continue to meet at Westminster to carry forward the discussions. Over the weekend of the Epiphany in January 1990, about sixty people met again at Prinknash Abbey. It was at this meeting that the decision to establish the Movement for Christian Democracy was taken. They based it on six principles that had emerged during the previous discussions; these were Social Justice, Respect for Life, Reconciliation, Empowerment, Active Compassion and Good Stewardship and they formed two committees, the first to draw up a foundational statement of the Movement's position and aims and the second to organise a conference at which the Movement could be publicly launched. The document now known as the '*Westminster Declaration*' was ready by early autumn and approved by 1,500 delegates at a rally in Westminster Hall.

The Movement began without media hype, and that was intentional. The founders wanted it to lay deep roots and establish solid foundations. There was also a considerable amount of thinking to be done. There has been no consistent lay critique of secularism in British politics and the Movement wished to develop one. At an early meeting the title of Movement for Christian Democracy was confirmed. Members wished to develop the Movement in the tradition of continental Christian Democracy, but they also wished to develop it with particular relevance to British politics.

The Movement is governed by a national Council with a steering group managing the day-to-day business. Membership currently stands at 10,000 with members living across the country from Cornwall to Shetland. The Movement has also started other groups to handle particular jobs and interests within the larger body. Policy groups bring together experts to develop the Movement's thinking and publish contributions to the general political debate. A Young Christian Democrats group provides a forum for political activity to involve young people. The Movement publishes its own newspaper, *The Christian Democrat*, every two months. It goes out to the membership by post and is also distributed in churches up and down the country. The circulation is now 35,000. The Movement also publishes policy papers and 'Epiphany' papers on subjects of general political interest, such as a study of personal debt in Britain, a look at how transport in the capital could be reformed and a new booklet on Christian Democracy from Professor Michael Fogarty. MCD holds four conferences a year including an annual conference, a summer school to look at the practical side of political activity and the Epiphany conference, which goes wider than the Movement's membership to look at the philosophical side of Christian Democracy.

The Movement was designed to influence Parliament and as its numbers have grown so has its impact at Westminster. The first campaign was on personal debt, but the Movement has and is engaged in others such as campaigning for full employment, opposing British donations to the Chinese population programme, and campaigning against gratuitous violence on videos. This last was particularly successful: after an MCD campaign in the country and pressure through the Parliamentary sponsor, David Alton, the Cabinet ordered Home Secretary Michael Howard to avoid defeat in the Commons and to promise to introduce legislation dealing with the problem. The Movement is also co-operating with other organisations to oppose the legalisation of euthanasia, and pressing constructive amendments to Bills on divorce and asylum. During elections the Movement gathers information for the voters on candidate views.

Overseas, Movement teams have visited Russia, Romania and Bosnia, and the Movement has its own charity, the MCD Trust, which works with projects overseas particularly involving children. MCD delegations also attend the major European Christian Democrat conferences. At home, the Movement has pursued initiatives to strengthen communities on the ground. There have been campaigns to launch Credit Unions and Mutual Guarantee Societies, common on the continent. Credit Unions provide a secure place to save small sums in local communities and obtain small loans without the need for people, many of whom are outside the conventional banking system, to approach money lenders at extortionate rates of interest. Mutual Guarantee Societies combine small and medium companies to pool resources to provide common services and to support each other against business failure. By guaranteeing each other, companies in an MGS are able to obtain finance from banks at lower rates than a single company would be quoted. In 1995 the Movement announced that it would be co-operating with the largest UK private advisor on debt to offer free assistance to those whose homes are threatened with repossession.

As the Movement grows so will its influence and its ability to change the system. Already its presence has had an impact within Parliament. As part of a wider revival among Christians of political activity it has contributed to influencing the warmer rhetoric emerging from all the parties towards traditional

Christian concerns. Turning into practice the rhetoric of values in education, supporting families or recognising a common morality that binds our communities together is the agenda for the future.

The contestants

It's accepted political wisdom that if you want to become an MP you must join a political party; the days of the slightest possibility of being elected as an independent disappeared with the Second World War. British political parties are strange beasts, and compared to their European or American counterparts look increasingly like political dinosaurs. In Europe parties commonly work together in coalition governments or as part of umbrella alliances. The process of striking deals and the day-to-day necessity of co-operation leads to a blurring of the edges, a mutual understanding that is foreign to our own system. In the States parties are vast loose coalitions that traditionally only have a role at election time. There has been a change in America since Newt Gingrich launched the Republican revolution, but in general an American politician's party gives as much indication of his policy position as the part of the country he hails from. Thus although a Democrat might be broadly liberal, a Southern Bo-weevil Democrat would be firmly conservative.

In the British system, party rather than ideology has been the dominating force. Yes, parties espouse a programme of views; yes, they can represent interest groups; but those views can change and each of the main party groupings is an often conflicting collection of political philosophies. Thus among the Conservatives you have a division between the right-wing Europhobes and the centre-left One Nation MPs, and in the Labour Party you have the division between the modernisers of New Labour and the class warriors of Old Labour. These interests are submerged in the party in the attempt to gain and keep power. There are few coalitions possible in the British political system. The first-past-the-post electoral system delivers governments with a majority of seats even if they have won only a minority of the votes. Credibility also plays a role. The parties must persuade the electorate of their fitness to govern, and the electorate tends to punish those parties which appear divided. For this reason discipline becomes essential, and differences within the party have to be covered up, smoothed over and hidden from public view. This task is the province of the whips, the party hard men charged with keeping the troops in line and snuffing out dissent and disloyalty. Conservative whips are working overtime at present to avoid any repetition of the defections to the Opposition that blighted the party's poll ratings in winter of 1995/6. Labour whips are also active muzzling the left, who have the potential to torpedo the party's high poll ratings if they slip the leash.

Then there are the minority parties, from the Liberal Democrats to the nationalists and the Northern Irish, each with its own agenda, normally regional. They also form alliances in pursuit of a specific aim. Thus the Scottish Nationalists provide a home for party members of wildly differing political views united in the cause of an independent Scotland. At election time these parties are joined by others, some long-established which have yet to win a Parliamentary seat, and others set up for the purposes of contesting the election. The Greens fall into the former category, the Referendum Party into the latter. Candidates such as those who represent the Monster Raving Loony Party join in to poke fun at the system and take advantage of the obligation on broadcasters to name all the candidates contesting a seat. The more po-faced politicians would like to see such candidates banned, and attempts have been made by upping the deposit required for contesting a seat to price them out of the election. These have so far failed, and those who decide election law have yet to try the alternative of requiring a collection of signatures before accepting a candidacy. It's my guess that the British public rather like having the fringe candidates and would take the view that whoever wants to compete for votes should be given a fair chance of doing so. But whatever your view, politics would surely be worse if there were no exhibitions of yogic flying from the Natural Law Party to entertain us at election time.

The Conservatives

The Conservatives enter the election as the underdogs, the favourites to lose. Moreover, serious doubts have been raised about their future existence as a party. This election for them is a make or break point. The fact that they have come to this pass is extraordinary when you consider that the Conservative Party is one of the monoliths of British politics. Conservatives have dominated Parliament since the turn of the century; they have formed more Governments over the last hundred years than any other party. In their own eyes they are the natural party of government.

But the party has never been in such bad shape. With unpopularity has come a sudden decline in donations from their traditional backers. The age profile of the party has changed dramatically: members are now more likely to be the old, and an active youth wing has virtually disappeared. On demographic trends alone the party is dying away. Their financial position is acute; it's always difficult to assess Conservative finances, which are deeply secretive, but most commentators estimated debts of anywhere between £12 and £20 million in 1995, debts which exceed the value of their London Central Office. Conservative associations are finding it difficult to raise their national quota for financial contributions and even more difficult to fund full-time agents. Tied to all this is a public perception that the party, after nearly seventeen years in power, is tired, fractious and no longer credible as a governing force.

There is another view, that the picture of decline and demoralisation is being reversed. Membership may be low, members may be old and constituency and national finances shaky, but this is merely a reflection of the national trend in politics. The British of the 1990s are not as keen as their parents and grandparents to join political parties, and as the election looms so the donations will go up. The networks of patronage and party resources are still all in place; given a favourable set of polls the situation could dramatically change.

The polls tell a mixed story. On the one hand Labour has never before maintained such a wide lead as in the last few years. On a whole range of measures the majority of the electorate consider Labour to be the more united, efficient and credible of the two major parties. On the other hand the polls also show that the Conservatives appear to have turned the corner and are now creeping up in the ratings. The rolling average from ICM polls shows that the Conservatives turned the corner in June 1995, when Major took on his critics and won the leadership contest. If that upward trend continues the Conservatives could just close the gap between themselves and Labour by the time of a May general election, with Labour a mere 1 per cent ahead on the adjusted figures. However, maintaining the upward trend at the same rate is going to be difficult. The Conservatives would have to rise faster and further than at any time since the election that followed the Falklands campaign. Whether or not they can do this remains to be seen; politics is a fickle trade where the unforeseen can wreak damage on the most likely of predictions. However, there is no Falklands war looming on the horizon to rescue flagging morale and the local elections prior to the next election are likely to see a massive Conservative defeat. As a result the Conservatives are increasingly targeting their message towards key interest groups, particularly the 43 per cent of the population who are mortgage holders. Their support has leached faster from the Conservatives than any other group and it is for that reason that the Chancellor has been concentrating on lowering interest rates to cut the cost of mortgages rather than reducing income tax.

The other criterion for success at the general election is that the Conservatives can heal or at least hide the cracks in party unity. For the first time this century political commentators have begun to prophesy that the party will split. The right has been ever more vocal in pressing its demands on the Prime Minister; the left, previously silent in the interests of party unity, has begun to imitate the right. In February 1996 the left are expected to launch their own policy statement which they hope will be printed by the party's publications arm, setting out their agenda for the nation's future. With a foreword from Peter Temple-Morris the group most behind this document is the Macleod Group of One Nation Tories which numbers about fifty MPs as its supporters. The right have attacked this initiative as 'foolish'; above all such a 'wet' agenda for Britain is not, they say, what the people want.

There is an argument that the nature of the party has irrevocably changed and that the right now have the whip hand in deciding the party's future. A leading proponent of this thesis is Julian Critchley, the old-fashioned Conservative MP for Aldershot. He argues that the social make-up of Conservative MPs has changed notoriously, describing the new Tories not as 'arrivistes' but as 'garagistes'. There appears to have been a definite shift. The right-wing groups have all seen increased membership; the Conservative Way Forward group's membership has quadrupled in five years from 500 to 2,000. In Parliament the '92 Group has seen membership rise from 60 to 100 in the same time. Observers on the ground argue that the new generation of hopeful Tory candidates are overwhelmingly right wing; nurtured during the Thatcher years they all defer to the individualist, Europhobic, free-market dogma of the period. Against this it can also be said that most of the Conservative high command would not fall into this group.

There is a theory that the Conservative party is riding an inevitable process of decline. Their enemies, the Communist menace, the left-wing threat, have vanished. No longer is it enough to say what they are against, they must now say what they are for. In an ideological vacuum the party has begun to put tax cuts as the prime objective and replace the demon of Communism with the fiend of the European Union. Neither is a suitable substitute. Tax cuts without massive state spending reductions are an economic nonsense, there is doubt as to whether or not the electorate would tolerate the wholesale dismantling of welfare networks, and Europe is not a credible bogcyman and a substantial portion of the party will not accept its demonisation. The internal logic of such a uniting philosophy is a party without the left, a party fiercely nationalistic and harsh on the weaker members of society. As he faces the next election not only must Major win but as a precondition he must rein in these tendencies within his own party.

The Labour Party

Aneurin Bevan once said that if ever Labour abandoned its belief in public ownership then the only conflict with the Conservatives would be about 'nuances, about semi-tones and half tints'. Well, under the leadership of Anthony Charles Lynton Blair the party has done just that, and far more. The major question surrounding Blair's remodelling of New Labour or even 'New Moderate Labour' as Gordon Brown has called it, is whether or not the baby has been thrown out with the bath-water: is Labour still a socialist party and if not, what is it?

Blair's achievement has been to capitalise on the work of his predecessors by performing a massive public relations change in Labour's presentation. I allude to the work of his predecessors because it was Neil Kinnock who faced down Militant and John Smith who took on the unions. Whether either of them aimed for the transformation in the party that Blair has built on both victories is one of history's great unanswered questions. Labour's ideological foundations have been torn up and reworked. A party to tax the rich? Labour will not introduce 'penal tax rates'. A party to launch a Keynesian boom in the economy? Labour would be 'fiscally responsible'. A party for comprehensive education? Grammars and grant-maintained plus streaming for the bright are all safe in Labour's hands.

The commentators confess themselves baffled. They search for policies that distance Labour from the Conservatives and find rhetoric instead: 'responsible', 'young', 'new' and 'caring'. Where's the beef? The answer proffered is 'stakeholding'. Yards of column inches have been spent telling us what stakeholding is, or ought to be, and yet it still appears elusive, a jelly of a policy approach that quivers and slides away whenever you think you've grasped it. The good news for Tony Blair is that it probably doesn't matter. The polling evidence suggests that Labour's policy announcements wash over the heads of the electorate without leaving anyone too wet. The public's perception is that the current lot in government are tired and ineffectual and that Blair is fresh-faced and able. Time for a change. The bad news is that this state of affairs is unlikely to continue for long. Sooner or later the spotlight will turn on Labour policies. Saying that you cannot confirm economic detail until you've seen the finances will no longer be good enough. Caution on Europe will require clarification. Can the party stand the strain?

This election is a watershed for Labour. Out of power for nearly seventeen years, they have run the gamut of public presentations, relaunches and policy appraisals. They can put up with Blair because he offers victory. If they lose, the party will not know where to turn. And Blair is singlemindedly pursuing his place in Downing Street and woe betide anyone or anything that gets in the way. Asked once what he could do for the poor, Blair replied that he couldn't do a damned thing for them if he wasn't in government, and as the left created in the autumn of 1995 he told them that they needed psychiatric help. This is the most dedicated attempt to win power in the second half of the century.

Blair and his modernising colleagues know that they are fighting on two fronts and the obvious battle with the Conservatives is the one that probably causes them least concern. It is the knife in the back from the comrades behind them that poses the biggest threat, for Blair's reforms are only skin deep. The modernisers know that in the past the majority of the Labour leadership and senior MPs signed up for public ownership, union power and every politically correct cause going. Now that they are passionate Blairites, one is left with the thought either that they have abandoned all pretence at principle in the search for power or that this is one of the major mass conversions in political history. Blair knows that out in the constituencies the same people are running the local parties and the Labour councils with much the same ideology as in years past. New members attracted by the warmth of a Blair speech are soon turned off by the frost in a local committee meeting. So far there have only been rumbles from the left. Blair's challenge is to keep the lid on the volcano until polling day. He is helped by the fact that the left want him to win; they'll then be in a better position to dictate terms. An eruption before polling day could reverse all the hard work of modernising since Blair became leader.

There's a similar sense of bafflement in predicting how a Blair government would differ from a Major government. The general consensus is that it will be a case of steady as she goes, and that Blair will accept the majority of the Tory revolution since 1979. Never again will the unions hold a Labour government to ransom; economic policies will be Conservative with the possibility of further retrenchment in welfare spending, Britain will be fractionally more Euro-friendly but still cautious, business will remain largely unregulated in the pursuit of foreign investment and corporate confidence, even constitutional reform may look less inviting in the cold light of the morning after polling day. It remains to be seen if Blair can keep the left down, convince the voters Labour has changed and skip through the scrutiny to come. If he succeeds, his transformation of the Labour Party from a moribund unpopular anachronism to a fresh Social Democrat option will be one of the political stories of the century.

The Liberal Democrats

The Liberal Democrats will enter the election with mixed feelings. Yes, they want to see the current government toppled; yes, they want the constitutional changes that Blair has hinted at, but they must be wary of their position in the polls. Recent tests of public opinion suggest that nationally they are down to about 14 per cent, a far cry from the percentages in the middle twenties which they racked up in the days of the SDP–Liberal Alliance. None of this will make much difference to their representation at Westminster. They will lose a few seats, particularly in natural Labour areas, and win a few, particularly in the South West, but Liberal Democrats have always done better when Labour is not on a roll. Now it is, they cannot hope for breakthrough at the next general election. None of this will stop Mr Ashdown setting up his stall for a hung Parliament. Such statements hype up any possible influence the Liberal Democrats may have, and the thing is never out of the bounds of possibility, given the vagaries of the current electoral system.

The Liberal Democrats benefit and lose from the vigour with which the other two parties pursue the battle against each other. They may bemoan the lack of media attention they receive but they also benefit from not having their policies put under the spotlight. This happened briefly in the first few months of 1995 and the experience was distinctly unpleasant. A paper, written for internal consumption only, on the state of the party's policies was given national coverage by the media. It provided a brutally frank assessment of their position, criticising policy as being confused, liable to damage crucial sections of the electorate and, in the case of GP fundholding, 'duplicitous'. If the Liberal Democrats had this sort of ammunition on their rivals it would feature on the front page of every election leaflet they produced. Expect to see a few choice phrases decorating the literature you receive as the election campaign hots up. None of this should do much damage on the ground; the received wisdom is that the Liberal Democrats have always been a touch too idealistic and there will be few who expect them to form the next government. They are the natural repository of protest votes, and the natural anti-Tory party in certain rural areas such as the South West.

The irony of all this is that the Liberal Democrats could wield more power with fewer MPs if the electoral system delivers the hung Parliament they desire, particularly if Blair needs their votes to curb the enthusiasms of his own left wing. But they should not be too confident that proportional representation (PR) is the key to a golden future. One scenario long avoided in Liberal Democrat circles suggests precisely the opposite. Under a proper proportional system of voting the face of British politics will change. New parties will be born as old coalitions collapse, voters will no longer be forced to accept the broad package of party policy which they have to accept at present. There will be more choice, and that may militate against the Lib Dems. As more groupings reflect wider policy positions so it becomes virtually unnecessary to register a protest vote. The Liberal Democrats could see their share drop to the level of most continental parties: about 6 per cent, although this may take some time given the size of the party and their large presence in local government. Certainly with a Labour Party led by a self-confessed 'centrist' their hope of occupying the popular middle ground in politics is waning.

The Greens

The Greens appear to be on the way out. At the height of their fortunes in the European election of 1989 they notched up 15 per cent of the vote and failed to win a seat. In the last two elections they fielded up to 400 candidates around the country. In 1997 they are likely to field a mere 70, the same number as in 1979, when they first stood on a national platform. The party has been rent with splits and scandals. Of their leading lights Sara Parkin has left, David Icke reinvented himself as the 'son of godhead' and Jonathan Porritt was almost expelled. According to their own estimates membership is down to 4,000, 203 of their local parties are in danger of collapse, a further third are giving cause for concern and the party expects to make a £30,000 loss this year. All this could just be turned around if Labour introduces PR. Meanwhile the Greens will be pushing their hope of putting environmental considerations at the heart of policy-making, running single-issue campaigns rather than changing the electoral landscape.

The Referendum Party

You've heard of Ross Perot and Silvio Berlusconi; now for the first time in British politics you have the opportunity to vote for a dyed-in-the-wool plutocrat intent on upstaging the establishment. Sir James Goldsmith, billionaire and French MEP, has a fortune secreted away in Liechtenstein and a Mexican jungle retreat, he is straight out of a James Bond movie and he means business. Having founded a Eurosceptic party in France, L'Autre Europe, he has now founded the Referendum Party in Britain. He has a war chest of £23 million and could cause considerable damage to the Tories. The sole aim of his party is to force a plebiscite on Britain's future in Europe. A Goldsmith government would pass one piece of legislation legitimising such a referendum and then call an election. The country would be run by a government drawn from all parties. In France, L'Autre Europe won 12 per cent of the vote and elected thirteen MEPs from a standing start. The first-past-the-post system is a tougher nut to crack but Conservative strategists fear that a vote as low as 1 per cent could cost them twenty seats, when every seat counts in fending off a Blair government.

The Socialist Labour Party

Love him or loathe him, one has to credit Arthur Scargill with an uncanny ability to keep in the public eye. But a talent to secure newspaper coverage matters less to Mr Scargill than loyalty to the true faith of socialism. Scargill reckons Blair is an out-and-out heretic, and so on 1st May 1996 he launched the Socialist Labour Party, a party based on 'class understanding, class commitment and socialist policies'. He hopes to fund the party from the unions, but this seems unlikely. He would need about £1 million to cover the electoral deposits he is likely to lose and his own union, the National Union of Mineworkers, is so strapped for funds that it failed to take part in the last Labour leadership election. This will not daunt Scargill, nor will the fact that many left-wing Labour MPS will have no truck with the breakaway at present. Nor should Scargill be written off yet. A Socialist Labour Party could get the boost it needs on the Commons benches if internecine warfare breaks out between Labour's right and left after the election. A long shot, admittedly, but one to keep an eye on.

The UK Independence Party

This is the creation of Dr Alan Sked, academic and fanatical Eurosceptic. It is the home of those Eurosceptics who are even more sceptical than Norman Tebbit and Bill Cash. Its aim is immediate withdrawal from Europe. There are not enough members or cash for this party to cause more than a flutter of interest. Incidentally, there is no love lost between Sked and Goldsmith. Sked described the Referendum Party as 'the politics of *Sunset Boulevard* practised by an ageing playboy plutocrat'.

The Natural Law Party

This one makes a reappearance after fielding a candidate in every seat in the final days before close of nominations in 1992. A wealthy religious organisation, it claims that 'yogic flying' can help cure all society's problems. Not to be confused with the Monster Raving Loony Party. This lot mean it.

Policy

Home affairs

The Home Office can be the graveyard of good intentions. With a brief spanning everything from law and order and prisons to constitutional reform, immigration and the media, it is at the centre of the political battle. Political theorists are generally agreed that the first duty of government is to promote justice, but how to deliver effective systems to tackle crime, defeat the drugs dealers and provide for prisoners can baffle the most assiduous Home Secretary. The current incumbent, Michael Howard, has had a rough ride, lurching from crisis to crisis and accepting notable setbacks on media regulation and prisons policy.

The Conservative position has been to picture Labour and the Liberal Democrats as soft on crime, unwilling to take the tough choices necessary to maintain law and order. This has been matched by Labour with some of the most tough statements of policy on crime ever made by those on the left. In the process Labour has outraged some of its own supporters, with Jack Straw taking flak from his activists when he pledged to tackle 'beggars, scroungers and squidgee merchants'. At times the debate has seemed to degenerate into an auction with each side attempting to convince the electorate that it is tougher than the other.

In the run-up to the election the Conservatives have also attempted to out-flank the Opposition. The 1996 immigration legislation, which sought to reduce the rights of refugees seeking political asylum as well as cutting their benefits entitlement, has been a case in point. For many commentators the Bill was seen as a thinly disguised exercise in pork-barrel politics, playing on the seamier side of national prejudices in an attempt to trap

Opposition spokesmen into an unpopular defence of foreigners' asylum rights.

The fear of crime

Two points ought to be borne in mind when assessing the parties' rival bids. First, the fear of crime has been on a consistently rising graph since the 1970s. Increased and lurid media coverage has had an impact on the popular perceptions of a threat to society.

A recent MORI poll recorded that nine out of ten people feel that there is a likelihood that they will become a victim of a violent crime. More than 25 per cent of those surveyed have given up using public transport or walking, and over 20 per cent avoid certain areas or streets, raising the worry that some parts of Britain are becoming 'no go' areas. More than half of those interviewed had not been a victim of any of the crimes covered by the survey over the previous two years. Respondents also emphasised the role of real-life crime programmes on TV aggravating their sense of fear. The fear of crime has not matched its prevalence in society, although some crimes, particularly those which are drug-related, have reached worryingly high levels. Moreover the reliability of crime statistics has been disputed.

Second, it is difficult to propose radical change in the law and order regime without incurring significant increases in costs. Rival party proposals on the Legal Aid Bill and the modernisation of the Prison Service, as well as the use to which new technology can be put, all cost considerable amounts.

Crime

The Conservatives have claimed that crime figures have shown a dramatic fall. In late 1995 Howard even claimed that 'the tide has turned'. The annual crime figures of that year recorded a 5 per cent fall in the number of offences, largely made up of fewer car thefts and burglaries, but the figures also included a slight drop in violent crime. Howard has gone on to claim that by removing criminals from the streets a tougher penal policy has also contributed to a fall in crime.

But these figures have been disputed. Although all sides of the political battle welcome any fall in crime figures, Labour has pointed out that the crime rate has doubled since 1979 when 2.5 million crimes were reported and that at a rate of decline of 3 to 5 per cent it will take fifteen years for the crime rate to reach its 1979 level. The Liberal Democrats have attributed the fall to targeted policing and community involvement and called for more of the same.

The most trenchant criticism of Michael Howard's claims on crime has come from academics and those working in the field. Oliver James, a clinical psychologist has attributed the fall to the decline of young people as a proportion of the population. He argues that car crime, robbery and theft are, in the main, juvenile crimes and the number of ten to twenty year olds has fallen by 17 per cent since 1987. The drop in reported offences overall actually masks a three-fold rise in violent crime since 1987. James attributes such rises to the growth of inequality and poverty in Britain, pointing out that in 1979 19 per cent of boys were brought up in low income homes compared to 30 per cent since 1990.

Other commentators such as Paul Cavadino of the Penal Affairs Consortium claim that the figures are also unreliable because the number of crimes actually reported to the police appears to have fallen. This may be in part due to a tendency among inner-city residents not to have home insurance, a disincentive to reporting theft. Cavadino has gone on to argue that the 25 per cent rise in the prison population is accounted for by less serious offenders on short terms and those who have been refused bail.

Conservatives
Michael Howard has been at pains to emphasise how tough he will be on crime. His policy announcements, which are likely to be repeated in the manifesto, have centred on harder sentencing. In 1995 Howard pledged a package including a British version of the US 'three strikes and you're out' system in which automatic life sentences would be handed down for those convicted twice of a serious violent or sexual offence which already carries a

maximum life sentence. Burglars convicted three times would be subject to a set minimum sentence and there would be an end to the current remission for good behaviour. Model prisoners would no longer be released after half their sentence but would serve 85 per cent of their time, while others would serve the full sentence.

Other initiatives, some of which may figure in a pre-election Bill, include: the confiscation of driving licences for non-motoring offences such as burglary or fine defaulting; a new maximum seven-year sentence for persistent drug dealers; a 'name and shame' scheme for offenders under seventeen; and backing for legislation to make stalking a criminal offence.

Howard has announced his wish to see some of these measures put through the Commons before a general election and at the time of writing the first steps towards this end have already been taken. A White Paper is expected in 1996 with a Criminal Justice Bill to enact its recommendations in the session beginning in November 1996. This session is likely to be interrupted by the general election and any legislation that has not received the Royal Assent by April will fall. It remains uncertain how far he is likely to get before an election given implacable opposition from some judges who are loath to lose their discretion in matters of sentencing. Any parts of his programme that he is unable to enact may well feature strongly in the manifesto.

It remains to be seen how effective such a package could be. It will certainly be very expensive and probably incompatible with tax cuts. In the last three years the prison population has risen from 40,000 to 52,000; an extra 12,000 prisoners would require a further 24 prisons at a cost of £1.5 billion, in addition to a further £23,000 a year in costs per prisoner. Some commentators have alleged that the whole purpose of Conservative policy in this area is to outbid Labour for the electorate's affections.

Labour

The Labour party has yet to produce a package of measures to compete with the Conservatives on prison sentences. This may well be due to Tony Blair's insistence on reining in his team and stopping them making promises which carry financial implications. That does not mean that Labour is not keen to be seen to be tough on crime. Jack Straw's attack on 'the winos and addicts whose aggressive begging affronts decent compassionate citizens' offended a broad range of lobby groups. Following criticism Straw toned down his rhetoric, but the Labour manifesto is still likely to major on an agenda to 'reclaim the streets' from vagrants and beggars.

Straw has also outlined proposals to 'nip young offending in the bud' by introducing two new court orders which would be designed to stop young offenders from sliding into a cycle of persistent criminality. The first order would require the offender to make reparation to his or her victim by working for them, if the victim wanted that, or for the community if they did not, over a period of three months. The second order would impose a three-month action plan of after-school activities concentrated on the offender's educational needs, while their families would receive support to help them with exercising parental responsibility.

Labour will further concentrate on tackling juvenile crime by introducing fast-track sentencing procedures for persistent offenders. Juveniles appearing in court will receive a 'final warning' on the first offence, thus ending the current practice of repeat warnings.

Such a scheme might well prove prohibitively expensive, but Labour has put a figure of £600 million on proposals for putting a further 3,000 policemen and women on the beat. The source of these funds is less certain. One proposal is that the money could be raised by cancelling plans being considered by the Conservatives for funding an identity card scheme.

Other more vague promises are that Labour will reform the criminal justice system, tackle drug abuse and introduce tougher penalties for crimes of violence or crimes involving guns. Labour has also promised a crackdown on those who disturb their neighbourhoods with excessive noise and those who deal in drugs. There is little detail and less costings for these measures.

Liberal Democrats
The Liberal Democrats, as in other areas, have an embarrassment of riches in terms of policies on law and order. Inevitably for

the party which pioneered community politics, there is much
emphasis on tackling crime through the community. The party
pledges to impose a statutory duty on local authorities to develop
'community safety policies' and would place a similar duty on
local planning authorities to consider the implications for crime
in planning applications. There would be local neighbourhood
crime audits to assess the services delivered by the police. The
pavement-pounding Liberal Democrats are also keen on as much
community policing as possible, promising 3,000 more bobbies
on the beat with increased local control of police resources. One
is left wondering how on earth tight policing budgets and drained
local authority coffers could ever cope with such an ambitious
programme. I have yet to find any costings.

Nationally the Liberal Democrats wish to create a Minister of
Justice with Cabinet rank and a new office of Public Defender
to sniff out miscarriages of justice. They would also establish
a Sentencing Advisory Commission to encourage parity in
sentencing policy. They are committed to extending legal aid
at a time when the Government is keen to put a brake on
its runaway costs and they also want to do away with the
mandatory life sentence for murder. Given these promises it
seems extraordinary that Jo Grimond's Liberals stood on a
platform to reduce bureaucracy.

The pattern is repeated when the Liberal Democrats turn their
attention to prisons. They want an independent agency to run
the Prison Service, greater concentration on community service
as an alternative to prison, and an increase in prisoners' rights
with personal case-workers for each prisoner, prison contracts to
set out their obligations and opportunities and a new Prisoners'
Ombudsman to review complaints from those inside. All this
would be magnificent in an ideal world, which is unlikely given
the current state of the economy and its probable shape after
the next election.

Conclusion

It remains to be seen whether law and order can be an election-
winning issue for any party, although the issue is of constant
and increasing concern to the voters. The Liberal Democrats

are open to criticism for the sheer Utopianism of their proposals while Labour can be criticised for cynically toughening their language without comprehensive costings. The Conservatives face the same charge, and reactions from the judiciary at their proposed loss of discretion in sentencing have been hostile in the extreme. It is a salutary reminder to all parties that despite some of the toughest rhetoric on crime in recent political debate a poll showed that only 15 per cent of the public had any confidence in the Conservatives' ability to deal with the problem of crime.

Immigration and refugees

It has been said that when the Conservative Party faces serious problems it reaches for the race card. Certainly the recent Immigration and Asylum Bill introduced into the Commons by the Home Office was widely seen as an attempt to disadvantage the Opposition by claiming that they were soft on protecting Britain from an influx of foreigners. It was unanimously condemned by the Churches as well as the pressure groups and agencies working with refugees.

Immigration policy in Britain has been driven by a mixture of fear of a deluge which the nation would be incapable of absorbing without horrendous social problems and worries about the likely costs of supporting so-called 'economic migrants'. The desire to end the influx of such migrants, particularly the Vietnamese boat people, led the Conservatives to establish massive holding camps in Hong Kong and then impose a policy of forced repatriation. Some of those threatened in this way committed suicide or self-mutilation rather than be returned to Communist Vietnam.

None of this affects Britain's obligation under the UN Charter to ensure that a place of refuge is provided for those who have a well-founded fear of persecution. But the process of claiming political asylum has been increasingly hedged about with restrictions and disadvantages. As the champions of those claiming asylum have continued to assert, it is difficult to obtain a visa from a crowded British consulate, negotiate your travel and arrive at Heathrow with incontrovertible proof of fear of persecution and all the correct documentation if the secret police are out to incarcerate and torture you. And yet the recent Immigration and Asylum Bill made the presentation of forged documents a criterion for refusing asylum. This is almost a Catch-22 situation: if a refugee is able to comply with current requirements for claiming asylum then he is probably not in need of protection.

There have been continual allegations that the operation of British immigration law is racist in the extreme. Certainly it is difficult to explain away the fact that 1 in 4 visitors from the Indian subcontinent are refused entry to the UK compared to 1 in 2,000 from the United States. A further 1 in 6 applications for settlement from India by wives and children of people already living in the UK are also refused.

The Conservative manifesto is likely to talk tough on immigration. If Labour's performance on the Immigration and Asylum Bill is anything to go by, it will soft-pedal the issue in the hope of not being branded likely to flood the country with immigrants.

Much of the debate is based on false preconceptions. Immigration rates have been in continual decline since the heyday of Asian immigration from East Africa. On the fall of the Communist regime in Russia, Conservative ministers warned of an influx of hundreds of thousands of former Soviet citizens keen to experience the joys of Western life. In the event the numbers admitted were in single figures.

There remains a final twist to the immigration debate. Hong Kong and its likely fate at the hands of the Chinese Communist regime will play an increasing part in the news in the run-up to the election. Giving Hong Kong to Communist China will hand millions of Hong Kong Chinese from a capitalist regime to a Communist dictatorship. Hong Kong's Governor, the former Conservative minister Chris Patten, has called for all those who hold British passports to be admitted to the UK when the colony is handed over. This won him few friends in the Tory Party. Labour, meanwhile, has kept silent on the issue. The Liberal Democrats would guarantee a right of abode to all UK passport-holders.

Constitutional reform

There's often more than a trace of self-satisfaction in some of the rhetoric used about the British constitution. Traditional commentators praise the flexibility of our unwritten constitution, despite the fact that it requires the services of several unappointed constitutional experts to interpret it for the rest of us. There is some difference between the descriptions of Barry's masterpiece by the Thames as the 'Mother of Parliaments' or the 'worst legislative slum in Europe'.

But in recent years there has been a growing sense of dissatisfaction, a feeling that systems dating back to the seventeenth century and beyond are no longer suitable for a twenty-first-century legislature. The first-past-the-post system has been challenged since 1900 by minority parties. What has changed since then is that electoral reform of various kinds is now supported by members of the major parties.

The Upper House of Parliament is ripe for reform. I cannot think of any other legislative chamber in the world occupied by right of birth rather than through winning an election. It is virtually impossible to find any serious politician prepared to defend the system on any other grounds than that it works in practice.

The feeling that the system is creaking is combined with a suspicion that a majority of our elected representatives are on a political gravy train liberally salted with perks, lush consultancies and well-paid directorships. The last session of Parliament saw the system groaning with investigations into bribery and corruption including alleged links with arms traders. The stock of politicians as a group has never been so low, plumbing the depths of the least-respected jobs along with estate agents and tabloid journalists. This association of political sleaze with a perceived need for political reform is even reminiscent of the early nineteenth century when Parliament went through its last major bout of constitutional change by abolishing rotten boroughs and extending the franchise.

But constitutional reform is by no means a certainty. Apart from arguments against change and the lack of consensus on any new system, there are also the vested interests of the politicians, the people responsible for inaugurating change. Self-interest has always been a powerful motivation in politics and it is unlikely that any political party would be prepared to sponsor any reform that they did not regard as benefiting their particular position.

There will be other pressures in play. The Liberal Democrat price for co-operation in any hung Parliament will hinge on reliable promises of reform. It would be unwise for Labour to antagonise potential allies by ruling out change. Moreover the current first-past-the-post system has a built-in disadvantage for any party scoring under 30 per cent of the vote. If the Conservatives were plumbing the depths of electoral unpopularity they could find the system that has benefited them in the past stacking the odds against Conservative candidates across the country. The so-called 'Canada syndrome', referring to the virtual wiping out of the Conservative Party as a parliamentary force at the last Canadian elections, might just be realised in a British election and that would change many Conservative views on electoral reform.

Electoral Reform

The current first-past-the-post electoral system has delivered Conservative majorities over the last sixteen years although the Tories have never won the majority of votes. In 1983 for example Labour secured 27.6 per cent of the vote and won 209 seats in Parliament. The Liberal Democrats scored just over two percentage points less than Labour yet won only 23 seats. In the 1989 European elections the Liberal Democrats, SDP, Greens and Plaid Cymru polled more than a quarter of all votes cast and won no seats at all.

Opponents of the current system criticise first-past-the-post for producing see-saw changes of government and policy on minor shifts in the vote. They claim it is divisive, polarising the political debate and increasing the temptation to indulge in confrontational politics. Supporters of the system claim that it is easily understandable to the voters, links MPs to a geographical area and provides for stable constructive government unhampered by the compromises inherent in the coalition governments produced by PR. Moreover, the first-past-the-post system tends to exclude the lunatic fringe on both right and left. It remains an interesting fact that when Britain has had to recommend an electoral system for countries coming out of a period of crisis, the supporters of first-past-the-post have invariably chosen a PR system. Thus Zimbabwe was given a proportional system at the end of its civil war and Northern Ireland had a PR system imposed for the European elections.

Party Policy

Conservatives
The Conservatives have no proposals for changing the current system, although there are individual Conservatives who favour PR. Such reticence could well be linked to the fact that the Conservative Party has been a major beneficiary of the current system. There have, however, been signs that the Conservatives might well consider reform for the Lords. Political commentators have said that the party must face up to the issue, given that Labour will almost certainly have a manifesto pledge to reform the Upper Chamber. As Parliament slides towards the election Lord Cranborne, the Conservative leader in the Lords, will be taking soundings among the inbuilt Conservative majority on what would be acceptable. Any proposals to reform the Upper House are likely to meet with opposition from some Conservative peers and the party is likely to keep any suggestion of reform as low key as possible. This may mean that it may stop short of a manifesto pledge of change and opt instead for the promise of a Green Paper on reform. Options being canvassed are likely to include hereditary peers being restricted in voting on some issues, the removal of voting rights from those who rarely attend, and the election by the hereditary peers of a group from their own ranks who will have full voting rights. The last option has the benefit of a constitutional precedent. At the Act of Union between Scotland and England in the eighteenth century, peers in the Scottish Parliament elected sixteen of their number to sit in a merged House of Lords.

Labour

In contrast Labour's proposals for reform of the Lords are specific but not without their problems. Labour is committed to introducing a Bill in its first year in power to remove the right of hereditary peers to vote. Labour would also set up a Royal Commission with the task of recommending a complete overhaul of the second chamber within two years. This strategy is bedevilled with ifs and buts. It is thought that the second chamber might be unable to function without the 550 hereditary peers; Tony Blair might well resort to creating the largest list ever of some two hundred working Labour peers to ensure that his government had a majority in the Upper House. Such radical reform would not serve the smooth running of the administration in the early years of a Labour government. One solution that has been trailed is that a number of hereditary peers will be offered life peerages to retain their expertise and co-opt them into the programme for reform. However, it may be wishful thinking to expect Conservative backwoodsmen to co-operate in their own extinction. Blair may revert to party dictat. In his 1996 conference speech he promised a reformed second chamber consisting of appointees who would probably be nominated by the political parties.

Labour's position on proportional representation has also kept observers guessing during the last Parliament. There have been consistent tensions in the party between those who favour and those who oppose a change. By 1991 there were two opposing groups within the party, both vigorously arguing their corners. However, a Labour working party chaired by Raymond Plant recommended the supplementary vote system for the Commons as well as PR systems for European elections, the Lords and a Scottish Parliament. The Plant Committee was then wound up suddenly before it could issue recommendations for a Welsh assembly and local government. Instead of opting for the Plant solution Labour has since toyed with the idea of holding a referendum on PR. Blair endorsed the idea during his campaign for the Labour leadership, but appeared to many observers to be lukewarm in his commitment to a referendum. Throughout the summer of 1995 there were reports that the idea of a referendum would be shelved at the conference. In the event these proved groundless: Jack Straw, Labour's constitutional spokesman, came out unequivocally for a referendum in Labour's first term. Meanwhile party policy is still committed to a form of PR for a Scottish assembly.

There have been rumours of other Labour plans for the constitution. Reports have emerged that Labour policy-formers are considering slimming down the monarchy. Front-bench spokesmen such as Mo Mowlem have called for an end to the Royal Prerogative, and Jack Straw is known for his view that the British Royal Family resembles a 'soap opera' and has called for a Scandinavian 'bicycling' style monarchy. Meanwhile papers have circulated in the Labour Party with proposed options for reforming the way the Commons works to ensure that Parliament could cope with the workload of the the first few years of a Labour government. Options being canvassed include a shorter summer recess, with MPS returning in September rather than October, and making Parliamentary Select Committees sit during the holidays.

Liberal Democrats

The Liberal Democrats have been long associated with the most radical proposals for constitutional change and a burning commitment to the cause of proportional representation. Their preferred system is the Single Transferable Vote (STV) in multi-member constituencies returning between two and seven MPs. The Liberal Democrats have argued for years that STV gives voters maximum choice and would produce a Commons that reflects the wishes of the electorate. They would also promote a massive programme of constitutional change, including the introduction of state funding for political parties to break the links between parties and vested interests, and fixed-term Parliaments to avoid the uncertainty they claim is created by the Prime Minister deciding the date of the election. The Lords would be changed into an elected Senate with Senators elected for a period of six years and supplemented by unelected members for additional expertise, and a Supreme Court would replace the Judicial Committee of the House of Lords. They would also reduce the size of Parliament with the Lords cut from 1,200 to 300 and the Commons cut from 651 MPs to 450. A Bill of Rights would be introduced with a UK Commission on Human Rights as an attendant quango.

The party also has the monarchy within its sights. In 1996 they pledged a reduction in Royal powers as part of a wider 'Great Reform' Act. The Queen would no longer have the right to choose the Prime Minister in the event of a hung Parliament, to approve treaties without Parliamentary consent or to set the date of the next election.

Conclusion
It is difficult not to believe that the moment for constitutional change has come. More thinking has been done and more promises made in this area in the last five years than in the previous two decades. However, no one proposal for change is without its difficulties and built-in problems. The Conservative decision barely to address the issue leaves the problems of the current system still festering. Labour's promise of a referendum on PR may appear to be progress, but any referendum can be undermined by setting awkward rules and Labour has not discussed the terms of the question to be put to voters. Reform of the House of Lords, despite the promises from the opposition parties, is likely to be a bed of nettles. It remains likely that if Labour win the election, constitutional matters will inevitably take centre stage. Labour is likely to face a sluggish economy with little room to increase government funds. If Labour is unable to deliver on its social agenda, a programme of constitutional reform has the attraction of making headlines at little cost to government funds. As a result Britain may well be on the verge of introducing PR for at least regional assemblies and possibly for the Commons itself. Such a development would sweep the old party certainties aside and open a new and very flexible era in British politics.

Foreign affairs

Europe

British foreign affairs are not what they used to be. We no longer wield the influence that we did after the Second World War; even our Gross National Product (GNP) has sunk to below the European average. And Europe, despite twenty-two years of British membership, is the demon that haunts political parties. In the 1980s the issue of Europe split the Labour Party and gave birth to the SDP. Now the Conservatives seem to be going through a similar phase. Europhobe can't stand Europhile, and Europhile responds by loathing Europhobe. For the first time in the last Parliament commentators seriously discussed the possibility of the Conservative Party splitting into a Europhobic Thatcherite right and a Europhile One Nation left. It remained an open question whether this would happen before or after the election.

The European Community was founded by the great Christian Democratic leaders of the immediate post-war period. Germany's Adenauer, France's Schumann and Italy's de Gasperi were determined that the horrific experience of a European war that had blighted the lives of every preceding generation should be stopped once and for all. The idea of mutual co-operation between nations and the pooling of national sovereignty for the greater good can be seen as one of Christian Democracy's greatest contributions to the world. The principles of the European Union come straight from Christian Democratic thought. Solidarity between classes, communities and countries is basic to any Christian Democratic programme and subsidiarity, that central value in the Maastricht Treaty, originated in a papal encyclical which attacked Fascist centralisation. The European dream of the founding fathers has become the orthodoxy of their successors, whether Social Democrat or Christian Democrat. In Europe the fight is no longer about the principles of the Union but about its future shape and organisation. The pursuit of purely national aims without reference to the aims of the European dream will win Britain few friends in a crucial marketplace and central political forum.

British attitudes to Europe have been shaped not only by our history but also by the propagandistic way in which both our politicians and our tabloid press have pictured the European Community. Britain has a schizophrenic attitude to Europe. The nation's heart may never be fully given to the European goal, but its head knows that we are irrevocably committed to remaining in Europe. In 1993 53 per cent of UK exports and 50 per cent of our imports were traded in Europe. Massive sums of European money have been poured into our inner cities, ailing industries, educational opportunities and training schemes. The thought of 'going it alone' without Europe spells economic suicide and would sideline Britain in the world community. Even if the electorate may relish anti-European rhetoric from our politicians there is a strong desire for a constructive policy to meet the European challenge. Whether or not our politicians can deliver such an initiative in the heat of a general election campaign remains to be seen.

Defence

The European Union has massive ramifications for British politics in all fields, whether economic, social or industrial. One element of the negotiations at the Intergovernmental Conference at Turin is progress towards a Common Defence Policy. Defence issues have lost the political explosiveness they had in the days before the Communist regimes fell. It is nowadays rare for the activities of the Campaign for Nuclear Disarmament to receive any coverage in the media. It is as though the issue of nuclear weapons has been overtaken by the end of the Cold War. Such a view would be hopelessly optimistic. If anything the new republics of the former Eastern bloc are less stable now than before the Berlin Wall came down; consider the republics of the former Yugoslavia. Many of them possess nuclear weapons and the number of countries acquiring access to nuclear weapons technology is increasing. Defence has always been seen as a prime responsibility of government, although increasingly our armed forces are only in action as part of peace-keeping efforts by an international force. Defence matters do not stop at the actions of the armed forces. Our defence industry is a major part of Britain's economy and one should not forget that Britain remains one of the top arms dealers in the world.

Overseas aid

Another responsibility is the country's overseas aid programme. There has been a tendency among all governments to put overseas aid at the bottom of the priority list. The aid budget is a soft target in economically tight times and the department concerned has been prey to those who would use it more to bolster British trade and exports with the Third World and those who are happy to thrust politically correct Western notions, such as population control, down the throats of the world's poor. Overseas aid is an emotive subject against a backdrop of the fact that the number of people in the world living in absolute poverty is likely to rise to 1.5 billion by the end of the decade. This is a subject that invariably raises its head at constituency election meetings up and down the country. Every party professes a commitment to the ideals of aid such as an eventual rise in the budget to the UN target of 0.7 per cent of GNP. But despite promises of such a rise no government has ever come close to the target. Britain has the unenviable record of donating less bilateral aid to the alleviation of poverty than most other OECD countries, and nearly a third of that aid is tied to trade or has other conditions attached.

Conservative Party policy

Europe
The national schizophrenia on Europe is mirrored with teeth in the Tory Party. The battle between those who support the

European ideal and those who are harshly sceptical has become a defining feature of modern Conservatism. Some of the most embarrassing moments of the recent Parliament for the governing party have involved disagreements over Europe. There have been back-bench rebellions, and threats of rebellions. At the beginning of 1994 the Prime Minister withdrew the party whip from a hard core of rebels and was then forced to climb down and admit them back to the parliamentary party as the threat grew to his majority. In the Conservative leadership election that year John Redwood stood on a frankly Eurosceptic platform; as he launched his leadership bid the television cameras recorded him flanked by the former Euro-rebels. As the Conservative majority came closer to wipe out so the Prime Minster found himself forced to straddle the competing factions. Besieged by both right and left on Europe and conscious of the populist appeal of an anti-European platform, the Conservative Party has adopted an increasingly sceptical tone on Europe. Such a tone was always likely to produce self-inflicted wounds. At the end of 1995 the Conservative backbencher Emma Nicholson quoted the party's opposition to the European Union when she defected to the Liberal Democrats.

Leading figures in the party have adopted differing stances. Kenneth Clarke, a champion of the pro-European Conservative left, while questioning the timetable for monetary union has also committed Britain to achieving the criteria for joining a single currency. Douglas Hurd, the former Foreign Secretary, a regular target for the right for his pro-European views while in office, has made his views clear since returning to the back benches. In his words, Europe 'is no longer an ideal for the high-minded. It is a simple statement of necessity.'

Meanwhile the Conservative Defence Secretary Michael Portillo was cheered to the rafters at the Conservative conference in 1995 with a tub-thumping Eurosceptic performance. He was pointedly congratulated by the Prime Minister on the conference platform in full view of the cameras. Ex-Thatcherite ministers, such as Lord Tebbit and Norman Lamont, have both urged the Government to distance itself from Europe. Tebbit called for Britain to withdraw from the European Court of Human

Rights in response to that court's criticism of the SAS killing of IRA members in Gibraltar.

The manifesto is therefore likely to be intentionally Eurosceptic, but some scraps will be necessary to keep the Europhiles on board. The balance is likely to be heavily influenced by the debates at the Intergovernmental Conference at Turin. So far Major has made it clear that a Conservative government in Britain would opt out of any moves towards a European 'superstate' if the Intergovernmental Conference presses ahead towards the goal of 'ever-closer political union'. The Eurosceptics will press for an assurance that a Conservative government will not take Britain into a single European currency if one is achieved by the target date of 1999. They are unlikely to succeed; keeping the party together on this issue will probably mean agreeing not to say anything on it in the manifesto. However, if it was felt impossible to ignore the subject a compromise solution would be to promise a national referendum before joining an EU currency.

One of the least covered aspects of the European debate has been the position of Conservative MEPs at the European Parliament. They have pursued a policy of alliance with the Christian Democratic grouping at the Parliament, the European People's Party (EPP). The Conservative Party made two applications to join the grouping as a political party member but was rejected on the grounds that it did not share the pro-European objectives of the EPP and advocated a regressive social policy by opposing the social chapter of the Maastricht Treaty. A compromise was cobbled together in the European Parliament whereby the Conservative MEPs were allowed to join the group as individual members on condition that they each signed a document committing them to EPP policy, which includes the federal goals of ever-closer political union, a single currency and the implementation of the social chapter. Each Conservative MEP signed the document.

It will be difficult for the authors of the manifesto to reconcile both Major's stated desire to be at the 'heart of Europe' and Conservative behaviour at European negotiations. In the latter he has largely been sidelined as a leader raising problems, doubts

and questions, many of them worthwhile at a technical level, but
without recommending any solutions of his own.

An Atlantic Community

One of the more dramatic foreign-policy shifts within the
Conservative Party over recent years has been the Conservative
appeal for a strengthening of ties with the United States. The
Major administration had come under attack from Mrs Thatcher
for 'allowing' the special relationship with the United States to
'cool to freezing point'. It would be unfair to land Major with
the blame on this point. Any decline in the special relationship
is more a matter of events than any neglect by the Conservatives
of Bill Clinton's Democratic government. Although Britain still
punches beyond its weight on many defence and security issues,
with the fall of the Russian Communist state the focus of
American interests has shifted from London to Bonn. There
have also been difficulties over particular issues, notably Bosnia
and Northern Ireland.

The Foreign Secretary, Malcolm Rifkind, has been floating
ideas for strengthening transatlantic relations since the party
conference of 1994. At that time he called for the establishment
of a chamber of transatlantic legislators. This was largely written
off as pie in the sky, but as Foreign Secretary his repeated
call in 1995 for a transatlantic trade alliance could not be so
easily dismissed. The idea has its attractions for those who
are Eurosceptic. Any dilution of the Eurocentric tendency of
the community is welcomed by them, which was why so many
supported the idea of rapid enlargement of the European Union.
But plans for a trade agreement linking Europe and the Americas
are not dismissed in the capitals of the continent. Klaus Kinkel,
the German Foreign Minister, has also called for an Atlantic free
trade area, and this call has been echoed by John Redwood. And
there has been strong support for the idea from the Scandinavian
countries and even from the European Commission.

Such an initiative unites the two guiding principles of British
foreign policy, the maintenance of NATO and the extension of
free trade. Rifkind's aim is to remove all remaining barriers to free
trade and thus create a single market of some 700 million people.

Investment across the Atlantic is said to be responsible for three million jobs on each side. One-sixth of Britain's exports can be accounted for by transatlantic trade. None of this is sufficiently well formulated for clear policy statements as yet. Progress will probably be made in a piecemeal way through Brussels, which has competence in matters of international trade. But commentators note that Rifkind is known for his personal belief that Europe's relations with the Americas will be a central foreign-policy issue over the next decade.

Defence

The Conservatives have always prided themselves on their reliability on defence policy, and regard it as an electoral asset. Deep in the Conservative mythology is an emotive patriotism summed up by the use of footage of Spitfires performing victory rolls over the white cliffs of Dover in a notorious party political broadcast in 1992. Conservative bullishness on nuclear weapons in the 1970s and 1980s was regarded as a major element in Mrs Thatcher's election victories, and one should never forget the importance of the Falklands factor in 1983.

With the fall of the Berlin Wall the heat has gone out of the defence debate but there are still outstanding issues between the parties. The Conservatives will try to portray the Opposition as soft on defence, although the emphasis has now shifted from nuclear weapons to whether or not a common European defence policy complete with a 'Euro-army' is a betrayal of British defence policy. The manifesto should contain an unequivocal commitment to NATO as the continuing forum for defence policy overseas.

But at the heart of policy as it affects the armed services and industry are the continuing financial stringencies forced on them both by economic necessity and the illusion of a peace dividend. While this is now at the heart of the debate on defence it is unlikely to cause waves during an election campaign. The Opposition has never been expected to promise increased spending on defence.

The British defence industry has been the only sector to escape the ravages of world economic recession. Britain sells arms aggressively with government backing. As the Scott Inquiry reminded us, we supplied arms to both sides during the Iran–Iraq war and saw some of our own exports turned against our own troops in anger during the Gulf war. The world of defence sales is secretive. The Conservative Government has pursued a traditional policy of refusing to give details of the trade when questioned. No party wants to be seen as soft on the arms trade and Conservative ministers, including the Prime Minister, have made noises about the need to judge the human rights record of the regimes with which we trade weapons. However, voters should consider whether or not these reassurances are honoured in practice. In a recent case the Conservatives wished to deport a Saudi Arabian asylum-seeker because his presence in Britain was thought to endanger a valuable arms deal, and there has been a long-standing campaign against the Conservative Government's willingness to sell arms to Indonesia, currently engaged in the oppression of the population of East Timor.

Overseas aid

The Conservatives' readiness to tie aid to trade has come under the scrutiny of the courts in recent years, notably in the case of the Pergau Dam. It is a link which has been consistently opposed by pressure groups and aid agencies. While the Conservatives, in common with other parties, have made a clear commitment to achieving the UN target for aid-spending of 0.7 per cent of GDP a year, they have never come close to achieving it and have even cut the aid budget, from 0.5 per cent of GDP in 1979 to 0.315 per cent in 1993; at the time of writing another cut is expected.

There has been much criticism, particularly from Christian groups, of some of the Government's priorities in aid spending. The Conservatives have pursued policies for halting population growth which have led to accusations that they are participating in population control. Over the last decade of Conservative government nearly £100 million has been given to the International Planned Parenthood Federation (IPPF) and the UN fund for Population Activities (UNFPA). Both organisations are notorious for their involvement in the Chinese Population Control Programme which is based on forced abortion and sterilisation of Chinese women. Baroness Chalker, the ODA minister, has vigorously defended the policy, arguing that by funding the IPPF and UNFPA the Government can influence family planning policy in China. This must be the only example of a government funding a human rights abuse on the grounds that by supporting it they can mitigate its effects. Since the Population Control Programme was introduced in 1973 there has been no evidence of any improvement in the desperate position of the victims. Further evidence of the effects of the notorious one-child policy caused considerable concern when the programme *The Dying Rooms*, chronicling the murderous abuse which abandoned female children are subjected to in China, was broadcast in Britain. The stir did not bring about any change in the Government attitude to funding the Chinese policy through the IPPF and UNFPA.

Labour Party policy

Europe
The Labour Party is now past its embarrassments over European policy which proved so disastrous to the party in the 1970s and 1980s. Moreover, given the political situation it is highly unlikely that those within the party who are still Eurosceptic will attempt to rock the boat on this issue as the election campaign begins. However, it is worth remembering that over the last thirty years the Labour Party has changed its mind about membership of the European Community seven times. It has taken the Labour Party nearly twelve years to shift from a Eurosceptic stance to a guarded pro-European position. The rationalisation for this process is intriguing. Robin Cook, Labour's shadow foreign affairs spokesman, has emphasised that Labour's previously sceptical stance was based on a perception of Europe as the preserve of capitalist industrialists and business interests. Now Labour perceives the European Union as a guarantor of greater rights for working people and an essential forum for the achievement of full employment and environmental improvements.

Labour is not uncritical of Europe. Although the party believes that it is inconceivable to end Britain's membership of the community, its policy is hedged with provisos and conditions.

It is harshly critical of the Conservative stance, arguing that Britain has been marginalised to a position of carping from the sidelines when we should be forming the agenda for Europe at the heart of the debate. Labour does not seek a federal superstate; instead it looks for a union of independent member states and calls for considerable reform of European Union institutions. Labour would open up the Council of Ministers, which currently meets in secret, to greater public scrutiny. It would boost the accountability of the European Commission to the European Parliament and give the Parliament greater powers over the budget.

Labour proposes a change in the Common Agricultural Policy to tackle the problems of waste and fraud by shifting the emphasis of payments to farmers from guaranteeing them a higher than market price for their produce, which encourages over-production, to paying them to manage the countryside. The party is keen on enlargement, seeing it as a guarantor of peace and stability in Central and Eastern Europe and an extension of democratic values and human rights to countries which have not enjoyed them before. But it is on social policy and employment that Labour really becomes a fan of the European Union. The party would ditch the Conservative negotiated opt-out on the social chapter, claiming that the argument that Britain would become less competitive is a fraud and that the chapter provides a level economic playing-field and an important guarantor of workers' rights. Labour justifies this stance by pointing to the number of British companies who have already voluntarily implemented the provisions of the chapter and the number of British firms who have eagerly bought European companies that are subject to the social chapter's rules. Moreover, Labour argues that by opting out of the Maasticht Treaty's social provisions the Conservatives have effectively abandoned their place at the discussions on the development of European social policy and Labour wants that place back.

On employment, the Labour Party proposes a variety of initiatives to boost jobs in the Community, including the establishment of a European Recovery Fund to use European economic muscle to promote infrastructure and training projects boosting jobs and skills. On the single currency issue Labour is more guarded. While accepting the benefits of removing the costs of currency transactions, currently amounting to some 18.5 billion a year, and creating a more stable economic environment for industry, the party has set criteria for joining the single currency that are tougher than those insisted upon by the European agreements. These criteria will have to be met before Labour signs up for the ECU. Robin Cook has argued that the longer a Conservative government damages the economy the longer it will take for British industry to achieve any real convergence with the economies of France or Germany. This could be interpreted as a Eurosceptic position, accepting as it does the possibility that a 'hard core' of European states will go ahead with economic and monetary union without Britain, and Labour has been careful to further emphasise its caution by saying that before Britain entered a European single currency there would have to be some form of consultation with the electorate. Not joining the single currency on time could have a damaging effect on inward investment and interest rates as Britain becomes economically as well as politically marginalised on the fringes of Europe.

Defence

New Labour has ditched most of its radical past on defence issues, and while the leadership may rejoice at the loss of yet one more electoral liability there will be some tears shed on the left for the end of the old idealism. In the 1980s the Labour Party went into elections committed to abandoning Britain's independent nuclear deterrent and with a deeply sceptical attitude to the defence industry and arms sales. For the next election the position will be almost entirely reversed. At the 1995 conference the party rejected a left-wing attempt to re-endorse a previous policy calling for the ditching of the Trident system. The vote was close, with 44.2 per cent of conference voting against the leadership line to keep the system. In the event Tony Blair's bacon was saved by the union block votes.

The justification for maintaining the independent nuclear deterrent is that it would be used as a bargaining counter in multilateral disarmament talks. In the words of Dr John Reid, the shadow minister for the armed forces, calls for scrapping Trident are 'pious slogans' and multilateral talks 'offer the prospect of Labour leading others to a solution', not 'sitting outside the conference room clutching a paper resolution'. Tony Blair has welcomed Labour's new commitment to the Trident missile system as an example of his party's new maturity. There is also the fact that scrapping the system would not result in savings of any great value: 95 per cent of the costs have already been spent. There is still some question over the number of Trident submarines that Labour would want to see in operation; however, Labour has ruled out taking a position on this before the next election.

If Labour's U-turn on nuclear weapons has surprised observers, its turnaround on the defence industry is equally significant – and equally depressing – for established Labour activists. Labour's shadow Defence Secretary, David Clark, has pledged the party to a new partnership with defence industries, arguing that they are crucial for Britain's overall manufacturing base as well as British defence interests. Labour would launch a strategic review with the full involvement of the military Chiefs of Staff. The objective of the review would be to prioritise British security needs so that the defence industry can plan for the future and invest for the long term.

For the remainder, Labour claims to be strongly committed to NATO while keen to see an increasingly strong 'European pillar' active within the alliance. An active peace-keeping role for British forces would be maintained. None of this suggests that defence spending will fall under Labour. There appears little prospect of a reduction if Labour endorses most of the principles of policy it has maintained under the Conservatives. This will still leave British defence spending well above the European average.

More surprisingly, Labour is now committed to supporting arms exports. Clark sees them as an essential component of the long-term prosperity of the defence industry. But aware that he is liable to the charge of putting British defence sector jobs before the human rights of the oppressed and tyrannised, he has also given the assurance that Britain under a Labour government will not sell arms to repressive regimes. However, it is worth remembering that it was Harold Wilson who sold arms to the military regime in Nigeria during Biafra's struggle for independence, and it was a Labour government that first sold Hawk aircraft to Indonesia.

Businessmen–ambassadors
An interesting policy proposal from shadow foreign affairs spokesman Robin Cook suggests that Labour would consider appointing businessmen as ambassadors in strategic markets. Cook has said that as Foreign Secretary he may appoint businessmen with 'experience, drive and flair' on temporary ambassadorial contracts to countries where they have special experience. Cook believes that such businessmen–ambassadors would have much to teach the Foreign Office about obtaining export orders for Britain. The Foreign Office did not dismiss the idea, leaving the intriguing prospect of Richard Branson in white tie and tails as our man in Riyadh.

The Liberal Democrat policy

Europe
The Liberal Democrat commitment to the European dream is unequalled anywhere else on the political spectrum. The Liberals and SDP Alliance were the most pro-European of the contenders in the elections of 1983 and 1987, and their faith in the Union and willingness to use the F-word when every other British political party has been shying away from any mention of federalism is one of the wonders of British politics.

Not that the Liberal Democrats are prepared to endorse anything from Europe. They wish to see a reformed European Union with a renewed emphasis on democracy and decentralisation. They would go along with everything that Labour has said on the importance of Europe for the creation of jobs, the protection of the environment and international security. They would applaud Labour's commitment to abolishing much of the secrecy that surrounds European institutions, but they would go further. The Liberal Democrats would aim to introduce a process of co-decision making between the Parliament and the Council of Ministers. They would want the Council to meet in public when it votes on legislation, they would make the Commission fully accountable to the Council and the Parliament and, of course, they are keen to see a uniform electoral system, in other words, proportional representation for European elections. The Liberal Democrats have also said that they will propose a new 'Marshall Plan' for Eastern and Central Europe, end the British opt-out on the social chapter and support an 'open trading' system, shorthand for a form of free trade. On the single currency they are pledged to 'moving in step with our European partners'.

There has never been much division in the Liberal Democrats on European policy but this does not mean that they do not have their problems. While their policies are closely reasoned and consistent, with hardly a whiff of fence-sitting, they may have the electoral disadvantage of ignoring the British passion for running Europe down. In the European Parliament the two British Liberal Democrat MEPs, the first to be elected at the last Euro-election, sit as members of the European Liberal Democratic and Reformed Group (ELDR), the union of continental Liberal parties. In many ways the British Liberal Democrats are an anomaly in this group, as one of its strongest members. Most continental Liberal parties are lucky to make the 5 per cent threshold for obtaining seats in their elections, and British Liberals outweigh them both in membership electoral performance and – often – seats won.

But the development of British Liberalism has been different from that of the continental parties. Liberals relinquished most of their Victorian free-market philosophy to the Tory right in Britain and developed a new ideology under Jo Grimond which could be called Social Liberalism. Not so on the continent; there, Liberal parties are often still advocates of a Gladstonian Manchester Liberalism that would find little difference with the economic thought of Margaret Thatcher. Many continental Liberals would feel quite at home with Norman Tebbit if it were not for his opposition to the European ideal; indeed the Conservative MEPs seriously considered applying to join the Liberal grouping at the European Parliament instead of the Christian Democrats. They finally rejected the idea on the grounds that they would not have significantly increased their influence with a small group such as the ELDR.

Defence

In the days of the old Liberal Party it was common to see the party leadership defeated by party activists on issues such as nuclear weapons. The new Liberal Democrats seem to have benefited from the fall in the profile of the nuclear weapons issue and their current defence policy is probably the most bullish they have ever produced. The Liberal Democrats argue that because of the increasing instability in the world defence spending should be maintained at current levels. They see little prospect of a cut in the defence budget and even argue that there may need to be a rise, depending on the demands on our armed forces.

On nuclear weapons, the Liberal Democrats support the retention of the Trident system but with only as many warheads as have been deployed on Polaris. A Liberal Democrat government would announce that it would only use the deterrent in response to a clear military threat, and they claim that a weapon of mass destruction could be used in a targeted way against military targets.

In terms of military priorities Liberal Democrats have a detailed policy, as one would expect of a party led by a former Marine. They wish to develop a Eurocorps including a British element with the emphasis on light armour and air-mobile troops able to be deployed quickly to crisis areas. But Liberal Democrats also see defence policy in the context of wider foreign policy and security issues. They would press for the establishment of a new UN information agency and introduce a permanent UN peace-keeping force with a military planning staff to advise the Security Council. They would favour preventive deployments to areas of crisis to stop escalation.

With Labour's U-turn on the defence industry, the Liberal Democrats now have the most radical and left-wing policy in this area. A Liberal Democrat government would regard a reduction in the arms trade as an essential step towards reducing world tensions. Liberal Democrats would ban the sale of weapons to nations in breach of international law and allow Parliament to exercise proper scrutiny over arms sales. They would call for the establishment of a European Union register of arms and, more crucially, reduce UK government support to the arms industry while developing alternatives for those firms engaged in the arms trade.

The Liberal Democrats' defence policy does lay itself open to the charge that it is idealistic in the extreme. Many of the initiatives would depend on international agreement. For example there is just no way that the Liberal Democrats can be certain that the UN would want, or have the resources, to develop a staff college for the training of officers in peace-keeping duties. Moreover, the wording of the policy on arms sales leaves it open to flexible application. The Liberal Democrats would strictly control the sale of arms to countries which abuse human rights, but strict control is not the same as refusing to sell to oppressive regimes.

Overseas aid

Liberal Democrat policy statements on overseas aid follow many of the radical and often politically correct notions that motivate the policies of other parties. Population is identified as one of the major problems to be tackled; the Liberal Democrats even regard it as a threat to world security. There is therefore an emphasis in policy statements on providing increased funds for family planning, particularly through non-governmental organisations. Much of this is likely to be channelled through organisations such as the IPPF and UNFPA, who are intimately involved in the oppressive one-child policy in China. I have found no Liberal Democrat policy statement that condemns the actions of these agencies or takes the Chinese to task for a population control policy in breach of the UN Charter for Human Rights. Stopping the people of the Third World from having the children they want is to ignore the real cause of the problem, the inequality of distribution of the world's resources, and tackle only the symptoms. It has always surprised me that western Liberals are so blind to the human rights implications of such a policy.

Much of the Liberal Democrats' policy outside this area is

challenging and useful, although one should read the small print which allows significant room for manoeuvre. Liberal Democrats would increase overseas aid spending 'towards' 0.7 per cent of GDP, but they do not promise to divert the necessary funds to achieve it within a given timescale. They advocate increased international co-operation on the problems of Third World debt and would work towards the complete remission of unpayable debts owed by Third World countries. However, much of this depends on international co-operation and they may find that other countries are less willing than the Liberal Democrats to remit Third World debt.

A note on landmines

One of the campaigns to catch the imagination of the British electorate in recent years has been the campaign to introduce a ban on the manufacture, stockpiling and trade in anti-personnel landmines and to get these indiscriminate killers banned under the International Convention on Inhumane Weapons. Christian aid agencies and pressure groups have been particularly active in this and there has been a sustained campaign of writing letters and lobbying MPs.

Landmines don't sign peace treaties. There are over one hundred million strewn around the conflict-ridden Third World, but a landmine does not respect the end of hostilities and they will go on killing and maiming the children and grandchildren of the soldiers who laid them long after the fighting has stopped. A further hundred million are stockpiled around the world ready for use because landmines are cheap, costing as little as $3 to buy. The same mine will cost between $300 and $1,000 to clear and make safe. Under UN estimates it will cost $33 billion to clear the current number of mines laid around the world. Landmines kill or maim up to two thousand people a month around the world. Civilians suffer most: farmers ploughing a field, women fetching water or children playing in the open air. Some mines are actually designed to look like toys and thus be attractive to children. Playing is a high-risk activity in an area laid with mines. Apart from their enormous cost in human lives and suffering, mines stop refugees returning to farm after peace is declared and are thus a major brake on restoring a war-torn country to peace and prosperity.

Britain has been ambivalent on the issue of mines. Its classification of weapons is confidential, and Government statements that there is a moratorium on the export of some mines do not fill one with confidence that all mines are covered by the ban. Certainly the Government has not placed a moratorium on the export of so-called self-destruct mines and Britain has been accused of upping the profile in these mines in an attempt to corner the market. Self-destruct mines are far from reliable. After the Gulf war the British teams clearing Allied minefields insisted on treating those laid with self-destruct mines in the same way as a conventional minefield. An estimated 1 in 10 self-destruct mines will fail and remain a danger long after the area is supposed to be safe. For the Opposition, Labour has refused all requests to make a policy commitment to introduce a complete ban on landmines.

Conclusion

We live in an increasingly interdependent world. The explosion in telecommunications, the need for international agreements on trade, the environment and security issues, all militate against the nation state. An economic disaster on the other side of the world can prompt panic in the markets of Europe. All this makes co-operation between states essential, but is there really any real difference between the policies on offer from the rival parties? On Europe, both major parties are sceptical about the single currency, more so on the Conservative side. On the future shape of Europe there is considerable agreement among the opposition parties with a great emphasis on a regional Europe. Perhaps at the end of the day each voter must ask themselves how confident they are in the credibility of each party. For example, both Labour and the Conservatives talk about consulting the people on the issue of the single currency but this need not mean a referendum. Both pledges would be considered honoured if the single currency was an issue at the general election.

Economic affairs

Economics for everyone

Discuss the economy and you have an instant recipe for confusion. There is a mystique about economic affairs that appears to rule out anyone except university dons or city high-fliers from commenting with any chance that their words will be listened to. The economic debate has become bound up with competing dogmas. It's as though you have to answer first the question of whether or not you're a Keynesian or a free-market follower of Adam Smith, Friedman and Hayek; and if you don't know what all of these great economists thought then you're not qualified to discuss the subject with the big boys.

The rarefied nature of economic debate is one of the great tragedies of modern politics, a tragedy because it is so unnecessary. We are not here to serve and bow before economic dogma and doctrine; instead economics is there to serve us. Part of the problem is the apparent separation of rarefied concepts, such as the narrow measure of the money supply, from the everyday realities of the economy. These obscure academic principles can often do more to confuse than clarify. Margaret Thatcher was broadly right when she implied that running the nation's economy was the same as running any household budget on a larger scale. Of course there are differences; countries don't tend to go bankrupt in the same way as people, but the competing claims of what we should spend on follow similar principles. Economics is a subject for us all and it affects each one of us.

The eighteenth-century writers and thinkers had a better insight when they linked economics to politics and talked of 'political economy'. The economy is not a subject in isolation from the rest of our political culture. Decisions on whether we should spend on roads or schools are intimately bound up with the political debate on transport or education. Political priorities are intimately informed by economic needs and the political debate revolves around competing visions of an ideal society. The fingers of economic policy stretch into every area of our lives.

No one deciding the priorities for their own household budget does so in isolation. Our spending decisions are inextricably linked to the society around us. How much the council will charge us for road sweeping, rubbish collection and the myriad of responsibilities that our local taxes subsidise has just as much impact on our spending and savings as the behaviour of our fellow motorists affects the premiums we pay for driving insurance. It's the same for a country's budget. We are part of an international community, and the behaviour of that community is inextricably linked with the formation of our own spending and investment plans. If no man is an island then in economic terms no country is an island, no matter what the geographers say.

One of the major differences between our view of the ideal household budget and our view of the way the national budget should be run concerns the vexed question of debt. If we are considering our own finances then we all know that debt can be disastrous. Whatever the size of our overdraft or our credit card bill we all aspire to a point when our income will match our expenditure, a balanced budget. We may take on loans to buy a car or fund a college course but we do so, hopefully, having made the judgment that the benefits of acquiring a car or a college education will eventually outweigh the financial pain of having to pay the bank back. It's the principle of Mr Micawber in Dickens' *David Copperfield* who remarked: 'Annual income twenty pounds, annual expenditure nineteen nineteen six, result happiness. Annual income twenty pounds, annual expenditure twenty pounds ought and six, result misery.'

One of the differences between personal finances and the finances of the country is that we don't apply the Micawber principle to the government. We may feel a sense of shock at the billions of government debt but the sums are too big to be real to us. We accept the fact that governments spend money they don't have, whether with the purpose of improving services or of cutting taxes before an election for popularity's sake. It is part of a government's business to manage the national debt. But of course, just like our personal finances, there is a price to pay for an unbalanced budget. If we are deeply in debt the banks get their revenge, and their profit, from lending us money at exorbitant rates of interest. So, if the government goes deeper into debt the financial markets push up the rate of interest on the national debt.

And there is a price to pay in the future. Just as an individual must scrimp and save and watch their spending to repay their personal debt, so a country will eventually have to pay. The timescales are longer, but if we pass our deficit on to future generations we pass the burden of paying for it on to them as well. Moreover, it is likely that future generations will have to scrimp and save even harder than us to clear our debts, because with the growth of the elderly as a percentage of the population there will be proportionally fewer people in work, a bigger bill to meet in caring for their pensioners, and thus fewer resources to pay off the debt.

They say that if America sneezes we catch a cold. In the States there is now a running row between Congress and the President over Congress's refusal to accept a massive budget deficit. Congress is not only using economic reasons to oppose Clinton's budget but it is also using a moral point. It is immoral to load the pain of our carelessness and poor provision on to the shoulders of our children. It is immoral for our government to spend money it doesn't have. So history comes full circle. Gladstone wouldn't have dreamt of introducing a budget that did not balance. The pressure is on for a return to the standards of a previous age and we can already see the effects in the Treasury's habit of producing forecasts, albeit optimistic ones, of when the budget will actually balance.

There is an argument for an exception to this rule and it runs along the same lines as an individual's decision to go into debt for the purpose of buying a car or that college education. There is a case for government going into debt by investing in the country to help it to produce more. Just as an individual may be able to earn a higher salary by acquiring more skills or a degree, so a country may earn more by improving its telecommunications or transport system. The decision to do this is a matter of political priorities and at the heart of the economic debate.

Napoleon commented sarcastically that Britain was a nation of shopkeepers, but in one sense all nations are. One of the ways in which as a nation we earn the resources for the government to tax is by exporting our goods and services to the rest of the world. In selling them the price matters, and the price is affected by costs of producing those goods such as salaries, National Insurance payments and health benefits. We live in an age when the free market has triumphed over the command economies of the Communist states. We are all free marketeers now, and at the heart of the debate on the market is the question of how much any government may interfere in the running of the economy. Only the politically eccentric believe that the government should never interfere. Virtually everyone believes that governments must regulate and tax if only to ensure that they can raise their own revenues. But there is a more important rationale.

The market has no conscience; it can be unjust, harsh and cruel. The market will not pay for the unemployed person who does not produce, or support the pensioner who does not work. The market can also be distorted by those who are prepared to try to twist it to their advantage and con the gullible or ignorant. To deal with these problems there has long been a consensus in British politics that governments have a right to intervene, regulate and tax to protect those dealing in the market, to redress any injustice and, through a national welfare system, to support those for whom the market will not provide.

The new economies of the Asian rim are challenging this orthodoxy. In Hong Kong, Bangkok or Singapore the government plays a minimalist role; there is far less taxation, regulation or welfare in these areas. The results have been dramatic, with massive growth and societies that are becoming wealthier than many well-established Western economies. As South East Asia grows in economic might so it will naturally export its economic values to the rest of the world. There are already those in British politics who point to the 'tiger' economies as a model which we should emulate. They talk darkly of the likely fate of any economy which cannot compete with them. But remember that we are discussing political economy, and that economic choices inform social conditions. I highly doubt that the people of the Western world would be able to cope with the conditions which the people of South East Asia endure: cramped living quarters, little or no welfare support and low wages. In the words of Edwina Currie, the reason these economies outperform the rest is that 'they pay peanuts and lock you up if you disagree with them'.

These international influences on our economy are now accepted by all political parties although there are differences in how we should cope with them. One market-oriented view would be that the situation will redress itself as the exploited workforce of South East Asia begins to demand the benefits which are available to the workers of European countries. As the Asian-rim employers and governments are forced to provide better conditions for their workforce so the prices of their goods will rise and the international economic playing-field will level. This explanation may ignore the cultural aspects that lie behind economic performance; it could be argued that the work ethic is more deeply imbued in South East Asia than in Britain, or perhaps Singaporean workers are more prepared to tolerate conditions which would have a European workforce out on instant strike. If this is correct it may take years for the market to level, with a lot of human misery in between.

Conservatives

John Major inherited the mantle of free-market Mrs Thatcher, and although it isn't difficult to find people who would argue that he has betrayed many of her principles he is still committed to lower government spending and low taxation as the key to economic success. But there is division on this within the party. The Tory right see the needs to reduce public spending and taxation as going hand in hand. Less government spending means less taxation means more money sloshing around to be invested for a successful economy. When asked about the impact on those at the bottom of the economic heap, right-wing Conservatives argue that more wealth from healthy economic growth is required and then the benefits of this will 'trickle down' to all levels of the economy. It was this idea that lay at the root of Mrs Thatcher's comment that the point about the Good Samaritan was that he had money to help the man who fell among thieves. Opponents of this view point to the nature of human greed and acquisitiveness, and wonder if any employer will pay more for a workforce than they have to. On the other side, One Nation Conservatives have a tradition of attempting to spread the benefits of the economy through society, particularly through competent welfare provision. Kenneth Clarke, for example, argues that workers in an advanced economy such as Britain need and want a high standard of publicly financed services, particularly at a time of economic insecurity.

All political parties need a big economic idea, an easily remembered soundbite that impresses the electorate and can be used as a convenient umbrella for a number of interlinking policies. For the Conservatives it is an 'Enterprise Economy'. Part of the fun for political commentators is to unpack such statements and try to see what they really mean; it's one of the ironies of life that politicians rarely spell it out. In the case of an 'enterprise economy', Major appears to be emphasising the need to liberate business from the shackles of taxation so that private investment in both the public and private sectors will drive forward national, and by extension individual, prosperity.

John Major has outlined the likely shape of a Conservative package in a series of speeches. At the centre of a likely Tory election strategy is the reduction of public spending, and that will mean 'tough choices' on spending priorities in public services. Major and the Conservatives would dearly like to see more services for people provided not by the State but by private enterprise and industry. The Conservatives argue that private provision is more effective and less bureaucratic than state provision, but of course it also means substantial savings to the public purse.

To forward this process the Government has launched the Private Finance Initiative, designed to link private companies into working with and providing for public services. To date the take-up for private finance schemes has been sluggish but Major has pledged that he will have contracts work over £5 billion signed up under the scheme by the end of the year.

For Major the economic priority is to keep spending and taxes down and to encourage business investment; the Conservatives point to the fastest growing economies of the world in South East Asia to justify this analysis. They also point out that while in the mid-1970s government spent up to 50 per cent of the national income, by 1995 the total was 43 per cent of national income, about 10 per cent below the European average. The Conservatives aim to get total government spending below 40 per cent of national income over the next few years. Critics respond that after seventeen years of Conservative rule the ratio of government expenditure to national income is at the same level as when Labour left office in 1979. Meanwhile national borrowing is still high and taxes are even higher.

The aim of reducing public spending below 40 per cent could prompt a range of policies depending on political priorities. At the current 43 per cent of national income, the Government is spending a total of about £289 billion. To take more than 3 per cent off this means that the Government needs to save some £12.5 billion. A government dominated by the right might rigorously enforce departmental budgets and not tolerate the spending departments overrunning their limits. Scrapping the Treasury's reserve of £3 billion would help, as would significantly reducing overseas aid, payments to Europe or pension payments to richest 50 per cent of pensioners. A government dominated by the Conservative left might cut back further on state subsidies for housing by abolishing mortgage interest relief, end the married couple's tax allowance, which has pointedly been allowed to wither in recent years, stop subsidising sectors of the economy such as farmers and students, and end tax relief on savings schemes which are the preserve of the richest people in society.

All these measures could contribute, but they are not the most popular of moves and are highly unlikely to appear in any Conservative election manifesto. Instead, as with any document, it's important to read the small print. What isn't said and what's left out can be just as important as all the promises included in the final text.

Labour

The accusation of economic mismanagement has been the millstone round Labour's neck. Time after time over the last sixteen years the Conservatives have managed to portray Labour as deeply flawed on the economy, and that strategy has paid dividends by frightening many people into voting Conservative. Perhaps the major political task that faces Labour is to shake off that image and win public endorsement of its capability to run a sound economy. And Labour has come up with a big idea and it doesn't stop at economic policy. The stakeholder democracy, or stakeholder economy – the phrases are used interchangeably, with 'society' sometimes tacked on the end for variation – is the soundbite intended to link policies ranging from the economy through to social provision and health care.

Tony Blair launched his vision of the stakeholder economy in Singapore and immediately fuelled a debate in Britain about precisely what he had meant. There had already been rumblings on the left that this was merely souped-up Thatcherism with a human face. On the other hand the Conservatives attacked the idea as merely a set of new clothes for the well-worn policies of Labour corporatism. New Labour commentators rushed into print to defend the idea and expand upon it. How much Blair meant of what they have made of the concept is open to argument.

In his original speech Blair talked of 'opportunity for all', stopping the wastage of talent, a fairer, more open society with social cohesion, a dynamic economy which involves everyone, an obligation of society to ensure everyone has a stake. Now this is the language of political rhetoric or political philosophy depending on how polite you are, but it doesn't spell out the means by which we reach such a Utopia. Some of the criticism of the idea was little more than political backbiting. To argue, as some Conservatives have done, that the 'stakeholders' would be the unions appears to misrepresent Blair's words, nor can it be interpreted as poaching Conservative clothes as a shallow rerun of a property or share-owning democracy.

Instead, Blair seems to be hinting that Labour would see government not as a universal provider, the corporatist element in Labour's past, but as an enabling body setting the standards for the market and encouraging wider participation in the economy. Thus many of the ideas that Labour is toying with, for example the introduction of private pensions for all, provide everyone with a 'stake' rather than the poor provision offered through the mess of the current National Insurance scheme. In his vision of a stakeholding economy Blair seems also to be hinting at a reworking of some of the ideas of industrial democracy, giving workers a stake in their employment. Under this idea companies become less of a profits-generating commodity but become communities – yet another example of Blair's fascination with communitarian ideas.

Much of this is attractive, new and a complete U-turn on former Labour ideas for the economy. Perhaps the one area where Blair dropped a heavy hint of policy proposals to come in his Singapore speech was when he said that Old Labour's ideas of the redistribution of wealth through the tax and benefits system were no longer appropriate; instead welfare should help direct people to a productive job.

The stakeholder-economy speech built on previous policy announcements from the Labour Party. Gordon Brown, the party's Treasury spokesman, had already called for measures to promote investment in the economy. Some of his suggestions have included the doubling of capital allowances, more incentives for long-term personal savings and a two-tier capital gains tax which would militate against buying and selling shares for a quick profit. Brown has portrayed himself as the champion of fiscal rectitude, keen to show that he supported the Bank of England's Governor, Eddie George, in his rows with Kenneth Clarke about raising interest rates. Brown has pointed to the huge bills of economic failure, such the £20 billion cost of unemployment; in that light getting people back to work actually saves the government money. More can be saved by keeping public spending under strict control.

There are numerous gaps in Labour economic policy at this stage. Getting the unemployed back to work requires investment which means finding extra money. Calls for fairer distribution of taxes remain just that; there are no details offered. Where the extra money will come from is a problem, particularly with Gordon Brown's assurances that there will be no radical hike in borrowing. Labour says that it cannot give details because it does not know in what state the economy will be when it wins the election, but this seems disingenuous: much of its proposed policies are structural and could be set out irrespective of the stage we have reached in the economic cycle.

Liberal Democrats

The Liberal Democrats have yet to find a soundbite. Somehow 'investment, partnership and sustainability' does not trip off the tongue, but it may be a good deal more descriptive than the efforts of the major parties. Given their internationalist perspective, the Liberal Democrats are unsurprisingly committed to working 'with the grain' of worldwide economic conditions.

They promise rectitude on public borrowing. Current spending will be separated from investment, and borrowing used only to fund the latter. In common with the other two parties, they want to promote savings by introducing a national Save-As-You-Earn scheme, but they have not been lured into flirting with the new ideas on private pensions for all and would replace SERPS with an obligatory occupational pension. The Liberal Democrats have always been in favour of an independent central bank, arguing that political control of monetary policy leaves it open to abuse such as unwarranted tax cutting before an election. They have now come up with a name for the institution to replace the Bank of England; under a Liberal Democrat government it would be called the UK Reserve Bank and would have operational independence with a mandate to keep inflation low.

As committed champions of regional policy the Liberal Democrats would want to regionalise economic policy, setting up regional economic development agencies and local investment banks. Together with increased powers for local authorities for boosting the economy, these would provide a more local feel to their hopes for economic regeneration. They would plan to help small businesses with legislation to penalise those who pay their bills late. The Liberal Democrats even include education as a crucial part of economic policy, arguing that the provision of a skilled and educated workforce is a central tool of economic progress.

Conclusion

There is a sense in which all three parties are struggling to push each other off the centre ground. There is a surprising degree of unanimity on the principles for running the economy. All three parties wish to encourage greater savings, all three are committed to keeping government borrowing strictly under control, all agree that a measure of deregulation will assist companies to perform strongly. What then are the differences?

At one level there are differences of emphasis. Thus a Liberal Democrat government's economic policy would have a regional dimension which does not rate a mention in many of the statements of the other parties. A Labour government could be expected to introduce a new view of how each citizen fits into their work and the society around them, while the Conservatives emphasise the need to reduce taxes and cut back spending.

The closeness of some of the rival policy statements produces some interesting observations. Conservatives have attacked Labour on the grounds that an increased social role for companies means, in effect, that Blair gets away from the need to raise extra government funds by transferring much of the burden for social welfare on to companies. Therefore Blair is the enemy of the business sector and economically irresponsible. Intriguingly Labour's proposal that companies play a greater social role almost echoes Major's call for increased private provision of public services. Conservatives would welcome the private provision for social costs, and Conservatives criticising Labour on these grounds risk shooting themselves in the foot.

At the end of the day the differences seem greater on the philosophical level than that of policy. The parties appear to arrive at the same destination by different routes. Labour broadly believes that proper social provision will produce a more efficient economy, while for the Tories a healthy economy will feed down to better social provision. Of course the economic facts are the same for all and unfortunately all parties will have to deal with a sluggish economy which cannot be operated in isolation from the immense international forces which help to shape it. Perhaps at the heart of the policy battle is less a struggle to impress the voters than a desperate attempt not to offer hostages to fortune by saying so much that they are boxed in by their own words.

Taxation

The political debate on taxation lies at the heart of the rival parties' bids for our support at the general election, and it is not the most savoury of political arguments. In the past there has been more than a hint of bribery about the different parties' positions, as though the electorate's votes can be bought if one party, normally the Conservatives, can offer a greater tax cut than its competitors. There has always been an element of this in recent elections and it has always been deplored by both political commentators and the party that was outbid, but there has been a significant change since New Labour appeared on the political scene. Now both parties are attempting to reassure us that everyone will be better off under their respective tax regimes. Only the Liberal Democrats have adopted the masochistic honesty of telling us what we all really know, that if we want better public services, and particularly a better education system, then we will have to pay for that with higher taxes.

Taxes are the fuel of government, the money that pays for its operation and the costs of centrally provided services from welfare to the armed forces. But taxes have also been seen in the past as a means of combating the injustice inherent in the unequal distribution of the nation's wealth. Those, and particularly the Labour Party, who wanted to ensure that more people had a greater share in the country's wealth saw taxes as a social mechanism of redistribution; by upping taxes on the rich the proceeds could be transferred to the poor through greater tax allowances and better public services. This lay at the heart of the battle of the classes that informed so many of the political debates after the end of the Second World War. Not that everyone who might have benefited subscribed to the views of the redistributors. Tory Chancellors have always been able to appeal to the greed or financial difficulties of many of those the redistributors were seeking to benefit by offering the promise of lower taxes and, in some cases, the illusion of greater disposable personal incomes.

There is a debate as to how heavily the British are taxed compared to our international competitors. It has been claimed that Britain has some of the lowest tax rates in Europe. According to Government statistics the average single British taxpayer pays 25.3 per cent of their disposable income in taxes and National Insurance payments. This is about half the European average. A similar person in Germany pays 35 per cent of their income in taxes, in Denmark 46.2 per cent and in the Netherlands 47 per cent. Direct taxation therefore appears to be lower than in Britain only in Spain, Portugal and France. Moreover, Britain has one of the lowest top rates of taxation in Europe, with highest earners paying only 40 per cent. In this sense Britain is not an overtaxed nation. However, this is only part of the picture. Britain taxes the low paid and those on average incomes much more highly than most other countries; the impression of a low average tax burden is because the wealthy pay so little tax compared to other countries. Thus despite the appearance of low average taxes a British production worker with two children and a wife at home loses the second-highest proportion of his wages in tax. In the Group of Seven industrialised countries (G7), only a German worker with the same circumstances loses more. In Britain the poorest 20 per cent of households pay 39.3 per cent of their income in taxes, while the richest 20 per cent of households lose less, at 35.2 per cent. Such a high tax burden might be expected to feed into improved social security provision, but only Japan in the G7 countries spends less than Britain on social security.

There is also a balancing act to be considered when deciding policy on taxation. At present the economy has a small but steady annual rate of growth and low inflation; we are hovering between a stagnating economy and an economy which can show signs of steady improvement. A tax-cut bonanza might endanger these benefits by hiking up inflation and sending interest rates soaring. High interest rates could damage the corporate sector by raising the price of borrowing for investment. Having said that, the burden of taxes on businesses is already remarkably low in Britain compared with other countries. In the UK the corporate sector contributes a sum equivalent to 5.9 per cent of GDP in taxes, nearly half the G7 average of 10.4 per cent.

There are two major factors that will influence the debate for the next election. The first is that politicians have significantly less room for manoeuvre on taxation than they are likely to acknowledge, and the second is that the Opposition has now joined the Government in a political auction for votes, each trying to outdo the other with promises on tax. The monumental nature of much of our public services, including free education, health care and an expensive system of benefits, means that it is practicably impossible to reduce significantly the burden of taxation in real terms. We live in a society with ever greater expectations and a lesser number of people able to pay for them. There is always a demand for higher spending on public services, greater provision for a growing number of pensioners, better educational facilities to match the revolution in technology, better and more expensive health care to take advantage of the rush of improvements in medical science. The pressure to increase public spending is inexorable, for we all feel shocked when we discover that a revolutionary and very expensive new cure is not available free to all in the National Health Service.

Against this background the Government is able to reduce taxes by the odd penny in a year when business profits, and thus corporate tax receipts, are up and public spending has been kept strictly under control, but this is a token tax cut, insignificant in the long term. Even if John Redwood's proposal of a £5 billion cut in public spending was all put into tax cuts it would amount to only about half of tax increases in recent years. Faced with this dilemma few politicians have had the courage to argue for either a real increase in the burden of taxation or swingeing cuts in public services. Instead there has been an attempt to shift costs to the private sector in the hope that the national tax burden can be reduced. None of this puts more money in the nation's pockets;

instead we increasingly pay for the same services as customers in the private sector rather than as beneficiaries of the Welfare State. Hence the emphasis on encouraging the private finance initiative of substituting public spending with private investment for the Conservatives, and the fact that the Labour Party is toying with a radical restructuring of the benefits system, with the option of taxing child benefit included.

The second major difference in the political battle at the next general election involves the Labour Party. For the first time in more than two decades the Labour Treasury team is attempting to outbid the Conservatives. In the past Labour shadow chancellors denounced their opposite numbers for attempting to bribe the electorate. Today Gordon Brown attempts to outbid Kenneth Clarke. Tax cuts have become the 'bread and circuses' of British politics.

Conservatives

Against this background and the Conservative Party's theme of an enterprise economy, John Major is likely to centre his appeal on taxation policy on a pledge to achieve the lowest tax rates in Europe. The Chancellor, Kenneth Clarke, has been clear about the objectives he is pursuing at the Treasury. Because it is highly unlikely that any of them will be achieved before the election, it is probable that they will form the core of Tory manifesto proposals. Clarke's package concentrates on the reduction of the basic rate of income tax to 20 per cent combined with a reduction in public spending to 40 per cent and keeping inflation under 2.5 per cent. As well as this the Conservatives have a long-term agenda for reducing both capital gains tax and inheritance tax, and abolishing the latter if possible. In Major's eyes capital gains tax acts as a disincentive to investment, and it has long been a Conservative article of faith that people should be able to pass on what they have earned to their children. According to Conservative thinkers, punitive inheritance tax acts as yet another brake on enterprise by diminishing its rewards.

The Conservatives claim that a basic tax rate of 20 per cent, lower than many of our international competitors, will mean that Britain will be able to attract the best scientists and top executives to transform industry into one of the most competitive and best resourced in the world. The low personal tax rate will be combined with a promise of low corporate taxes, which the Conservatives again hope will act as a magnet for international investment and make Britain the preferred location for foreign companies establishing themselves within the European market-place. Combined with many of the Conservatives' other pledges to keep government regulation of industry at a minimum, lower costs to companies and increased investment in skills training, education and the transport infrastructure, it could almost be suggested that the Conservatives consider that Britain has to emulate the Asian-rim tiger economies to compete effectively. But not all is sweetness and light; pursuing such a policy will mean severe cutbacks in public spending and many of the choices to be made in this field will not be wildly popular with the electorate. The Conservatives have made it plain that 'tough choices' will have to be made but have not yet outlined precisely which services will feel the edge of the knife under a re-elected Tory government. To a certain extent, talking tough on the difficult choices to be made can be disingenuous. It implies that no one is trying to pull the wool over the eyes of the electorate and provides a suitable penitential feel to discussions about national extravagance.

We have an indication of where cuts will be concentrated. Major has said that the education budget, the National Health Service and law and order spending are all sacrosanct. This suggests that the biggest cuts will be concentrated on welfare provision, and Major has made a point of saying that the typical family pays up to £15 every week to keep the benefits system running. These proposals have not been greeted with unanimous enthusiasm by the parliamentary party. The Conservative MP who defected to Labour, Alan Howarth, remarked that the proposals to cut taxes were 'not decent'. Major has been quick to reply that he does not believe that business will take the risks and be properly committed to his vision of an enterprise economy unless the incentive of high personal rewards is there. The equation for the Conservatives is simple: lower taxes mean greater investment in industry, and the greater the investment the more jobs will be produced.

Labour has attacked Tory proposals on tax as impractical, falling short of their objectives and unlikely to help their popularity ratings in advance of a general election. Labour maintains that popular disenchantment with the Conservatives would persist even if taxes fell to 20 per cent. Moreover, the Chancellor would have to find an extra £10 billion to return personal taxes to the point at which they were three years ago.

Labour

The Conservatives hope that Labour can be portrayed as a prisoner of its past, a high-tax, high-spend party which, unable to raise the sums necessary to fund ambitious welfare proposals, is forced to tax the majority of the population at rates which alienate the electorate. It has been one of the major tasks of New Labour to change this perception of the party, and to some extent it has been successful. New Labour no longer presents itself as the party of higher taxation for greater social benefit; instead Labour claims the mantle of the party with the best ideas for restructuring taxation in such a way that we all benefit. The economic package to achieve this is complicated and further clouded by the fact that Labour has tried its best not to flesh out the policy proposals with too many details. It argues that these cannot be given until it has some indication of the state of the economy it will inherit after winning a general election. There is also more than a hint of promises made which will only be honoured in the right circumstances. It remains to be seen if Labour can deliver such conditions.

Labour spokesmen have been cautious of offending any one group in the rush to secure wide electoral backing. Much of the impetus of policy announcements has been concentrated on reassuring groups who would expect to suffer under a Labour government. For example, Labour leader Tony Blair has repeatedly said that he sees no need to return to the penal tax rates of 80 or 90 per cent that were imposed by the last Labour government on the high paid and wealthy. These, he claimed, are gone for good and he echoed Conservative rhetoric on the need to reward hard work, risk taking and success. This does not mean that taxes would not rise for the high paid. But Blair has said that any proposed rise will be announced before a general election. Commentators suggest that it could mean hiking top tax rates from 40 to 50 or 55 per cent.

On savings Labour is keen to encourage personal saving as a means of increasing investment in the economy and broadening the base of savers by increasing incentives. Gordon Brown has floated a variety of ideas that may feature in the manifesto. Labour will continue to support the principle of saving through PEPs and TESSAs by introducing a new Individual Savings Account to further promote long-term saving. The new account will be targeted particularly at those planning for retirement; there would be tax allowances payable after a period of years and designed to encourage people to keep savings in for the long term. Labour will also consider extending tax relief to those putting savings into building society accounts, with the aim of encouraging more people on lower incomes to save. At present tax brakes on savings schemes particularly benefit those on higher rates of tax.

Perhaps the most controversial of Labour's policy proposals has been the idea of introducing a lower-rate income tax band of 15p in the pound in the first term of a Labour government, with the aim of achieving 10p in the pound as a long-term objective. Combined with adjustments to benefits policy, this could make a heavy dent in the so-called poverty trap, where many of those on benefits find that they lose more of the social security payments than they gain in pay by taking a job. The Conservatives have dismissed this proposal out of hand as the world of 'fantasy economics'. Academic criticism has been more constructive. The Institute of Fiscal Studies has pointed out that the cut would be hugely expensive, costing up to £8 billion, and suggests that introducing a new lower tax rate is not the best way to help those on benefit or those seeking to escape the poverty trap. Under the current system of benefits, where family credit and housing benefit are paid to those in work, the combined tax rate can amount to 96.85 per cent, a massive disincentive to taking a job. A 10 per cent tax rate would cut this to a hardly distinguishable 96.4 per cent. The Institute for Fiscal Studies argues that by far the best way of helping those on benefits and low incomes is to raise personal allowances; this would eliminate tax because the size of the allowance would exceed income, a massive incentive to take a job. The Institute further points out that of the fifteen million adults on the lowest incomes most, such as pensioners, pay no tax at all and therefore would not benefit from a 10p rate. Labour has since argued that the reason for concentrating funds on a lower tax rate would be to avoid passing the benefits on to the wealthy, who would also benefit from higher tax allowances, but this problem could be solved by reducing the higher rate tax threshold to ensure that the wealthy still keep their share of the tax burden.

In 1996 Labour came up with an answer to those who claimed a 15 or 10p rate was too expensive. To fund the cut, Labour would reverse previous Conservative cuts in the rates for inheritance and capital gains tax.

Labour's other major proposal on tax is to cut the rate of VAT on fuel from its current rate of 8 per cent to 5 per cent, the lowest rate of VAT on fuel allowed under European Union rules. Such a rate would save the average family about £32 a year at a cost of some £480 million. The Conservatives have recently seen imposing VAT on fuel as a useful money spinner. The 8 per cent rate was introduced in 1994 and subsequent Government attempts to increase it to the full 17.5 per cent were defeated by a back-bench revolt. Heavy heating and lighting bills affect particularly the old and the poor. The Labour Party have been coy on how this proposal would be implemented. At first Gordon Brown said that it would be a priority for the first Labour budget; other Labour officials have said that the proposal is not a firm policy commitment and would only be implemented if the money was available. Labour spokesmen have refused to say where the money would come from to replace the £480 million cost of the policy. In January 1995 the Labour Party refused to support a Scottish Nationalist amendment to the Finance Bill of that year to cut VAT on fuel to 5 per cent.

Labour has not escaped criticism from within its own ranks on its taxation proposals. A few years ago both the rhetoric of economic stringency and the promises of going soft on taxing the rich would have been booed at any Labour conference. With the need not to rock the boat and hamper chances of winning the next election, major criticism of taxation policy from within Labour ranks has been left to disaffected senior members of the party such as the former deputy leader, Roy Hattersley. Hattersley has been uncompromising in saying that Labour cannot achieve the social reforms it desires without hitting the wealthy with tax rises. He argues that it is dishonest to maintain that the poorest section of society can be helped without massive redistribution of wealth and that somebody is going to have to pay for this. If 'BMW owners' are going to be penalised to help the poor, Hattersley would want the party to come clean on this and start the process of convincing some of those who would have to pay more that this would be both worthwhile and desirable.

Liberal democrats

After the frenetic Dutch auction between the two major parties in convincing the voters that each will tax less than the other, the Liberal Democrats have adopted a position, rarely seen in politics, of proposing higher taxes, specifically a 1 per cent rise in income tax to pay for improved education. They echo some of the preoccupations of the other parties, they share the view that the tax system should encourage enterprise and savings, but they add that the tax system should be open and honest and based on the ability to pay. The party claims also to be committed to the free market, competition and the tight control of public spending. It has set tax bureaucracy firmly within its sights. It further recommends the merging of the taxation and benefits systems. As a result the Liberal Democrats now have the most radical tax policies in British politics.

On personal taxation, the Liberal Democrats would merge income tax and National Insurance contributions. National Insurance, originally intended to contribute to a fund for all, has been abused by successive governments spending the money as soon as it is raised. As a result no effective fund has been established; however, no government has been willing to end the fiction of contributing to such a fund because the public might perceive the move as a rise in income tax. The Liberal Democrats would take up to fifty thousand of the lowest paid out of tax altogether, presumably through a modest increase in allowances. They would introduce three new higher rate tax bands starting above the current ceiling of 40 per cent but not exceeding 60 per cent. The top rate would be applied only to those earning in excess of £100,000 a year. Liberal Democrats would abolish TESSAs and PEPs and instead, in a system that merges tax and benefits, introduce a tax credit for the first part of tax due on investment income. They would replace inheritance tax with an accessions tax, which would assess the ability of the recipient of a legacy on their ability to pay rather than the total level of the legacy. Although the Liberal Democrats share the other parties' distaste for Mortgage Interest Tax Relief At Source (MIRAS), they are the only party committed to its abolition; even so, they would introduce a new mortgage benefit to target help to those on low incomes.

In 1996, the Liberal Democrats set out what they called a 'tax contract' with the electorate. This includes the provision of tax statements showing where our taxes go. They also promise voter consultation on marginal taxes such as the duty on tobacco. Voters could tell the Government what they think by filling in questionnaires; participating in telephone referendums or logging in on public access computers. Of course, Liberal Democrat ministers would not be bound by the results of such a consultation.

The Liberal Democrats have been criticised for unreasonable spending promises. Labour in particular has suggested that a package which includes a commitment to raise taxes is an electoral liability. The Liberal Democrats have argued that voters will respect a party that is honest about its intentions on tax and that the hard fact is that you cannot have better public services without paying for them. Ashdown refers to personal taxation as the price for membership of a civilised society.

Summary
Taxation policy is hedged about with provisos and conditions in such a way that assessing the different proposals put forward by the parties becomes little more than an act of confidence.

All parties are committed to increasing investment, but in different ways. For the Conservatives, initiatives to increase investment concentrate on attracting funds to a high-profit, low-cost economy. The emphasis of Labour statements has been to encourage savings by a broader range of the national population through incentives for all to save in special schemes. Liberal Democrats, although committed to abolishing the current schemes, argue that their new tax credit on savings and linking the ability to pay to taxing savings will encourage more people to invest in the economy.

In the same way all parties are committed to keeping a tight rein on public spending. Both Conservative and Labour look set to target public services by transferring many of the costs currently borne by the public sector to the private sector. Liberal Democrats are pledged not to let spending exceed the tax take and to borrow only for infrastructure investment. Promises on tax cuts are more difficult to assess. How confident can we be that the Conservatives' basic rate of 20 per cent or Labour's new lower rate of 10p in the pound are anything more than hopes rather than firm promises? There is certainly an air of unreality about the pledges that have already been made to the electorate. We all know that more money for the things that society needs has to come from somewhere, but there is a distinct tendency in the two major parties to avoid giving the impression that anyone will have to pay.

Politicians are hemmed in by the facts of life in our economy. Radical restructuring is necessary if we are to break the current cycle, and there are few proposals on the table that come close to what is needed. Announcing the home truths involved is regarded as meat that is too strong for the electorate to take. Nor will any of the proposals effect a massive redistribution of resources to the poorest 30 per cent in society. Perhaps these areas will be fleshed out in the manifesto, and as polling day approaches we will be given more details of the costs involved and more of the gaps will be filled in. But don't hold your breath. The record of British politicians of facing the unpalatable truth on tax is not good, particularly before an election.

Employment

Work is a defining feature of our lives. Not only does it provide an income but it sets a pattern and rhythm to life as well as providing a major part of the social interaction that makes us members of the community around us. The availability of stable, secure employment is the foundation upon which all of us would like to build our lives, but since the mid-1970s this picture of life and society has become less and less the case for more and more of our fellow-citizens. The issue of employment bridges both those who are unemployed and those in work, for increasingly as we approach the millennium those who are in work do not have the security their fathers and grandfathers enjoyed. We live in the notorious 30/30/40 society, with our adult population divided into 30 per cent who are economically inactive, 30 per cent who have unstable and insecure and often ill-paid employment, and 40 per cent who still benefit from a relatively secure job at a good rate of pay.

Of all British men, 1 in 4 are now unemployed or economically inactive. Nearly half of these are between fifty-five and sixty-five years old, the men who have been declared 'redundant' or have retired early, and who make up about 21 per cent of the working population. The unemployed make up 8 per cent of the workforce, 4 per cent of them out of work for over a year, and the position has become steadily worse. In 1979 6 per cent of British households had no member working; by 1994 this percentage had risen to 16 per cent. This is the 30 per cent of society where the underclass is to be found, those with no hope of regaining a job, marginalised in their communities, with their relationships under pressure, facing a daily slog to maintain a level of subsistence.

Then there are those at the bottom of the employment pile. The 1980s and 1990s have seen their jobs become less well paid, less secure and more highly pressurised. With the deregulation of much of the former body of employment law and the growing demands on employers to produce fatter profits in a shorter time, the workforce has borne the brunt of the changes introduced in the name of 'efficiency'. More workers are now on short-term contracts, uncovered by much of the social protection available to those in full employment, self-employment has doubled over the last decade, and there has been a massive increase in part-time and casual work, as women have flooded on to the job market and been hired to do jobs at a cheaper rate for their employers than the full-time male employee who would have done similar work in the 1960s and 1970s. Of all new part-time jobs, 70 per cent are for fewer than sixteen hours a week, and these jobs do not qualify for sickness benefit or holiday entitlement. For more and more of our population such part-time employment plays a central role in household income. These jobs are insecure in the extreme. As with those on short-term contracts, such workers have little or no protection against dismissal if the employer needs to cut costs for greater profit. Family breakdown, repossession of the home, getting by on tight budgets supplemented by high personal debt: this is the risk-laden world of the insecure employee.

The 40 per cent at the top of the employment pile are relatively well off. They are those working in full-time tenured jobs covered by the remainder of employment legislation. They have unions to guard their rights and the full catalogue of benefit entitlements and paid holidays. But their number is shrinking by 1 per cent a year as we press ahead with contracting-out and the breaking up of the big institutions such as government service or the great companies. For them as for all those in work the pressure is on to maintain their jobs under a greater burden of hours worked in the knowledge that there are many who would step into their shoes if they fail to make the grade. British workers work the longest hours in Europe; two-thirds work more than 40 hours a week, the European target, while a quarter work more than 50 hours, an increase of between a quarter and a half since 1984. As a result 44 per cent of the workforce reports arriving home exhausted, and according to the Government's Chief Medical Officer 1 in 3 workers report being under stress at work with 1 in 7 suffering problems as a result.

From 1995 the Movement for Christian Democracy has been running a campaign to promote full employment in Britain. Every political party claims to be committed to such a goal and the purpose of the campaign is to encourage and hold meetings in the fifty most marginal constituencies for the electorate to hear the rival party proposals on fighting unemployment. Full employment is not an unachievable goal. For twenty-five years after the last war unemployment in Britain stood at a mere 2 per cent largely made up of those transferring from one job to another. Countries such as Japan have a similar level of unemployment today. The battle against structural unemployment is a matter of political will. The Movement bases its campaign on the Christian understanding that work is a God-given benefit to man. When this element of the creation order is ignored it causes extensive disruption.

Family breakdown has often been associated with financial insecurity, and such insecurity is now a daily feature of our working lives. Crimes against property show a close correlation with unemployment rates; Dickenson in *Crime and Unemployment* (Cambridge 1994) estimated that for every 10 per cent fall in unemployment there would be a 4 per cent fall in the number of offenders. There have also been links drawn by other studies between unemployment and suicide and drug offences. MCD itself has proposed a package of measures to all parties calling for the tax and benefit systems to be merged to tackle the unemployment trap, where the tax implications of accepting work act as a disincentive, for co-ordinated wage bargaining to tackle the inflationary spiral created by 'leap-frogging' wage claims, and for a job guarantee scheme for the long-term unemployed.

The implications of the employment environment for the government are equally serious. The unemployed take from the national finances in the form of benefits; part-time and casual staff do not contribute the tax that a full-time employee does; the growth in unemployment and insecure work ups the benefits bill. Unemployment costs the Government some £20 billion in benefits and lost taxes even before the statisticians attempt to quantify the costs of ill-health, crime and relationship breakdown associated with unemployment and insecure work. Employment has risen speedily up the league of issues which the electorate considers most pressing, and remains one of the major tasks for any political party aspiring to government after the next election.

Conservatives

The Conservative Party in recent years has considered unemployment as a problem closely associated with the international situation. The worldwide recession, combined with the impact of the new technologies and the need to compete with countries without the costs of Britain's Welfare State, are all blamed for the rise in British unemployment. On this analysis government intervention to create 'artificial' employment is pointless and can indeed be counterproductive by loading more costs on both the state and the corporate sector and making them even less competitive in global markets. From this analysis the logical step to reducing unemployment is first to reduce industry's costs through deregulation and to concentrate on making industry as competitive as possible. As British industry achieves a commercial edge so it will expand, creating more prosperity and more jobs in its wake.

This does not mean that the government has given up on providing help to those seeking jobs – there are the political pressures of being seen to be doing something to tackle the problem – but initiatives have centred on training schemes and job-getting skills. The former tackle the skills and education gaps produced by the new demands of technology on business and the latter seek to provide job seekers with the ability to make the most of themselves in a highly competitive market.

In the past unemployment was not seen as a problem that affected Conservative voters to the same degree that it impacted on Labour support. If mass unemployment was concentrated in the mainly northern industrial heartlands of the Labour vote then the Conservatives could count on employment not being an issue that affected their own support. It has also been alleged that the party was reluctant to tackle unemployment because a highly competitive job market meant that prospective employees would be more pliable in accepting the loss of their job benefits and social protection as well as lower rates of pay. The existence of mass unemployment, and the fear of those in the job market of joining the ranks of the long-term unemployed, would then act to assist the drive to make Britain competitive. The British workforce needed to accept the same conditions as the workers of Malaysia and Hong Kong if they were to compete effectively.

However, there has been a marked change in the distribution of unemployment since 1991. The recession began at that point to bite into Conservative areas, with white-collar workers being hit for the first time in large numbers. Unemployment in areas of the country that normally vote Conservative rose five times as fast as in Labour-voting areas. But unemployment in Conservative parts of the country was far less long-term overall than in Labour constituencies. After 1992 unemployment fell twice as fast in Tory areas than Labour. As a result the amount of unemployment has spread more evenly across the country. Labour areas now account for 49 per cent of total British unemployment; Conservative areas account for 43 per cent. This is no longer, if it ever was, a one-party problem, and the political pressures can be expected to be reflected in the manifestos.

The Conservatives are also very conscious of the cost implications of long-term joblessness. As a result proposals for a scheme of 'workfare' have been trailed for possible inclusion in an election manifesto. The idea emanates from the Downing Street Policy Unit, formed by Mrs Thatcher to spearhead the radical reforms she introduced and to second-guess the Civil Service; under Major it still fulfils a central role in providing policy initiatives and back-up to the Prime Minister. Workfare envisages offering jobs to the long-term unemployed on the pain of them losing their benefits if they refuse to take the job. There are several pilot projects already in existence. From the Government's point of view, one of the main advantages of such a scheme is that it cuts the soaring cost of unemployment benefits; it may also make inroads into the black economy. Government advisers point out that spending surveys of the unemployed show them spending more than they receive in benefit, suggesting that many engage in casual work without declaring the income. A workfare scheme might force those on the register to declare undisclosed income. The Treasury has criticised proposals for workfare because it believes that there will be high start-up costs to introduce the scheme. Workfare has also been opposed by many employment pressure groups on the grounds that it provides government-subsidised cheap labour which undermines the jobs of many on low incomes.

It is likely that party strategists will also announce new initiatives to help the unemployed find work. There are now twenty-one separate schemes in existence and the newly merged Department of Education and Employment has been pursuing initiatives to increase their effectiveness. For example, it is hoped to introduce the new Vacancies, Opportunities and Providers (VOP) database to all jobcentres during the course of 1996. The new system, at a cost of £700 million, will match vacancies to job seekers faster than at present. Legislative changes and benefit changes such as the job-seeker's allowance have been introduced to place more obligations on the unemployed to hunt for a job.

Conservative statements on unemployment will also point at the sustained fall over the last two years. This growth is almost entirely in service sector jobs and has been broadly welcomed by all sides of the political debate, although with reservations concerning the speed unemployment is falling and the need for more investment.

The manifesto may also include new proposals for inhibiting strikes in public services. In the wake of Post Office and London Underground strikes in the summer of 1996, the Conservatives are considering depriving unions of their immunity from being sued for damages by the public. New rules would apply to 'monopoly public services' and the strike would have to be 'disproportionately damaging' to the public. There are problems with this policy. It's difficult to define a 'monopoly public service' and more difficult still to construct a 'proportionality' test for the courts.

Labour

Labour faces a quandary on employment policy. The party is committed to full employment, but New Labour is also concerned not to terrify employers and others who might have to pay the costs of achieving it. The party has a history of close – some would say too close – relations with the trade union movement, a relationship which Blair has attempted to redefine. Many of the unions now advocate policies considerably to the left of the parliamentary party, and Blair will not want to be tarred with the same brush as them. Finally Labour must find a strategy for getting people back to work which does not offend its own left wing but is seen as economically responsible by the electorate. Blair has been outspoken on the 'special relationship' with the unions. Within the party he has backed moves to restrict the power of the union block vote at the party conference. He has told the unions that they will not have preferential access to a Labour government, nor any more right to be listened to than employers. The whole tone of Blair's comments has been to distance the party from the close links with militant unionism that caused so much suspicion and concern in the past.

The unions themselves are going through a crisis in both role and membership. Unions in Britain have a proud record of pressing forward workers' rights, pay and conditions, but our unions did not develop in the same way as their continental equivalents. By the 1970s they were a modern version of medieval overmighty subjects and the Thatcher governments set out to break their power once and for all. They succeeded beyond their wildest dreams, and the star of British unions has never been so low. To cap it all, in the wake of the Nolan report into sleaze in Parliament their right to sponsor Labour MPs has been called into question.

As their fortunes have changed so unions have sought to redefine their own role, seeking contacts and influence outside socialist circles and beginning a debate on extending their role to helping part-time workers and the unemployed, groups which were previously excluded from the benefits of union membership. At its 1995 conference the TUC set out priorities for the future. These included a universal right of representation for every worker, unions to be consulted by the employer on any issue which involved 10 per cent of the workforce and full union recognition where a majority of employees vote for it.

It would be premature to assume that Labour's special relationship with the unions is dead. It was the unions who helped Blair to his conference victories in 1995; they provided a useful antidote to left wingers in the constituency sections of the party. In the next election the unions are expected to provide most of an estimated £10 million for Labour's war chest and will be providing equipment and activists for Labour target seats. Critics of the party have alleged that the Labour leadership has in secret promised that a new Labour government will pursue an 'agenda for rights at work' including measures on union recognition and 'lawful solidarity action'.

At the heart of Labour's appeal to the electorate on employment is a commitment to tackle the problem of low pay through the introduction of a minimum wage. At present, more than a million people earn less than £2.50 an hour; a further 2.5 million earn less than £3.50 an hour, and another 4.7 million earn less than the £4.15 an hour that most commentators feel is the highest figure that could be set. At present all other European Union states have introduced a minimum wage, ranging from £4.68 in Luxembourg to £1.81 in Greece.

The Labour Party has hit problems on the minimum wage within its own camp. The left wants to see a figure set before the election, and wants it to be high. There are also several other questions raised by Labour's proposals for setting a level. There is a wider debate about whether or not a minimum wage alleviates or aggravates poverty. Within the party the left has pointed out that opinion polls show that it would be popular for the party to announce a figure before the general election, and that two-thirds of those questioned would like to see the figure set above £4.00. A figure of this order would benefit 4.5 million workers, while a figure set under £3.40, the figure set in the 1992 election manifesto, would benefit only half that number. A more realistic figure is probably £3.33, and there have been several leaks, dismissed by the party, which claim that the front-bench team is aiming for such a figure.

The New Labour strategists argue that to set a figure before the election would be to hand electoral ammunition to the Conservatives; the higher the eventual figure set, the more a minimum wage will be open to the criticism that it destroys jobs. Among the formulae bandied about for setting the amount, the most popular is half male median earnings, but there have been disputes about whether or not part-time workers' earnings should be included in the male workers' pay for the benefit of the calculation. The Labour leadership is keen to tie employees and unions into supporting the final figure and is committed to setting up a Low Pay Commission to negotiate the rate if they win the election. The left argues that such a Commission will merely provide a forum for delaying implementation.

There are further problems with the detail of the policy. Although the Labour leadership currently has the backing of the party for a policy of not setting a figure before the election and deciding it in the Commission, there have been further questions raised on the workings of the Commission. A third of its members will be independent of both unions and employers, and they are likely to have the casting vote in reaching a decision. No details have yet been released on how they will be chosen or who they are likely to be. There is also a fear that the introduction of the minimum wage will spark a round of high pay claims to maintain differentials, with several unions pledging support for such claims.

The second prong of Labour's employment policy is a package of measures to get the unemployed back to work, with a special emphasis on the young. Labour will introduce a national network of career bureaux, linked into computers to help people move back to work. This is hardly new. Most of the ingredients are already on the ground in the form of jobcentres likely to be equipped with the VOP system by the time a Labour government is formed. At the most it amounts to a reorganisation of existing resources.

The package for the young unemployed, those under twenty-five, will be funded by a £3 billion windfall tax on the utilities, and aims for the abolition of youth unemployment. Under the details of the scheme young people out of work for more than six months will be offered four options: work with a private-sector employer, who would get a £60 a week tax rebate for every young person employed on condition that they are given day-release training on an approved course; work in the voluntary sector where they can still claim benefits but receive an extra £20 a week and a day's vocational training; work with a new environmental taskforce for six months while receiving benefits and £20 a week; and finally approved training courses, maintaining their rights to benefits.

This package has been costed by shadow Chancellor Gordon Brown at £1.4 billion, of which a billion would be spent on the package for the young in the first year of a Labour government, and would hope to provide work and training for up to 700,000 young people. Previous Labour pledges include paying £75 a week to any employer hiring any unemployed person who has been out of work for more than two years and the abolition of the sixteen-hour rule, whereby anyone who receives more than sixteen hours' education a week cannot claim benefits. The Labour Party hopes that the package will pay for itself within five years through a falling benefits bill and rising tax payments.

There is an element of compulsion in Gordon Brown's plans which has lead to an accusation of introducing workfare. Under the scheme, a young person who refused to take one of the four options within a month would lose 40 per cent of their benefit indefinitely. This is the first time that the Labour Party has ever promoted benefits penalties, and has produced rumours of shadow cabinet rows in the press.

There have been criticisms of this policy from outside the Party. Overseas experience of such schemes is mixed. Brown claims that between 50 and 70 per cent of those on similar schemes abroad are kept on by their employers; others point out that other European countries with such schemes have higher rates of youth unemployment than Britain at present. Some economists argue that subsidised jobs inevitably displace unsubsidised jobs and that the knock-on effect of the implementation of such a policy would be to put an older generation out of work.

The Labour manifesto is also likely to include proposals for a 'citizens' service' aimed at up to 100,000 unemployed sixteen- to twenty-five-year-olds. Those on the service would be set to work in the community in hospitals, residential care schemes and environmental projects. They would keep their benefits, be paid expenses and might gain a qualification at the end of their service. The £30 million annual cost would be funded with the proceeds of the windfall tax on utilities.

Liberal Democrats

The Liberal Democrats approach the problems of employment with a two-pronged attack concentrated on achieving full employment and increasing the skills of the working population. The Liberal Democrats point out that their proposals for investing in the infrastructure and education would in themselves create jobs, albeit mostly only for the duration of the investment boom. They would also introduce a benefits transfer programme, where the long-term unemployed would have their benefits paid instead to an employer, who would then be obliged to provide training. For youth unemployment they offer a volunteer scheme under which young people without work could commit up to two years to community service. Their new Regional Development Agencies would develop strategies for increasing employment in their own regions. The Liberal Democrats also offer a minimum wage, but one set at a regional rather than a national level; they imply that this is likely to be lower than any figure that Labour decides on and attack the Labour Party by claiming that Labour's broad brush approach – they would set the same level in Newcastle as in London – would cost jobs.

On training, the Liberal Democrats would entitle all sixteen- to nineteen-year-olds to two days' training a week. They would impose a training levy on companies equivalent to 2 per cent of their total payroll minus whatever they spend already on training. They go on to say that they would give every adult the right to a period of retraining or education at some point in their working life.

On workers' rights the Liberal Democrats would introduce legislation setting out what each employee can expect. Each employee would be given a contract of employment, and discrimination in rates of pay depending on whether or not a worker is a member of a trade union would be outlawed. Workers would be entitled to appoint a trade union to represent them by a simple majority vote. To deal with problems of low pay, the Liberal Democrats would establish a Low Pay Commission to recommend a regional minimum and allow local authorities to require their contractors to pay rates equal to those in industry.

Summary

At the heart of the debate on employment is a difference in the view of how the economy works. The right in British politics has always maintained that government interference in creating subsidised jobs is likely to be counterproductive and that the only real improvement can come from improving the competitiveness of industry. For the left this is a counsel of despair, condemning millions to unemployment and more to conditions at work which emulate the worst of overseas sweat-shop employment. It is certainly the case that conditions at work in Britain lag behind our European counterparts. The question is whether the sacrifices made and expected of our workforce justify the improvements to our economy from the laissez faire regime, and the answer to this question depends on which measures you believe are the best for assessing British industry. But for many people the employment issue is a question of morality, and any system which condemns people to a life without work or a decent income and constant insecurity, whether as a result of the policies of right or left, is frankly immoral.

Industry

Not so long ago it was an accepted truth of politics that businessmen supported the Conservatives. From the fat cats in the boardroom to the more cerebral industrialists at the CBI, industry backed the Tories. Nothing is that simple any more. In 1995 *The Times* quoted a spokesman for the British Institute of Management as saying 'the Government's traditional close ties with business are coming apart at the seams'. Meanwhile Conservative Party coffers are more than usually empty as industry donations fall, and some companies are even beginning to invest in the Labour Party. There are a number of factors behind the change. Industry has felt the pressures of the recession as much as individuals, times have been tough and demands for results pressing, and inevitably the Government has attracted some opprobrium from the fallout. Second, Labour has been engaged in a political public relations effort aimed at industry without parallel in its history. The notorious 'prawn cocktail circuit', begun under John Smith's leadership, a process of meeting and wooing the bosses of British industry, is paying dividends.

The extent of business dissatisfaction was revealed in a 1995 survey by the Institute of Management. The results showed that more than half of all managers thought that the Government was out of touch with the needs of business, and this was reflected in a swing of 18 per cent in voting intentions from Conservative to Labour. The Institute survey reveals that British managers are predominantly pro-European, echoing the comment of the chief executive of one of the UK's largest engineering firms after hearing the anti-European rhetoric at a Tory conference: 'Someone should remind these people where we have to do business to survive.' Of all the managers, 53 per cent were opposed to a referendum on Britain's future relationship with the European Union, although 51 per cent were against closer political union and 46 per cent against the introduction of a single currency.

The figures mask a difference in priorities between big and small businesses. It is the small businesses that are concerned that adoption of the social chapter and a minimum wage will damage their prospects. Big business tends to be more sanguine. Whatever the differences within business, industry, and the City establishment that exists alongside it, remains a core audience for any political party serious about being elected in 1997.

The problems facing the industrial sector are considerable. There are the issues of competitiveness and European policy that have been mentioned elsewhere but there is also the structure and system for business in Britain. The buzz word in recent years has been 'efficiency', the objective the maximising of shareholder profits. It is in the name of this programme that much of the restructuring of British industry has been carried out in the 1980s and 1990s. Companies need investment to develop and expand and that investment, particularly for the larger companies, comes through stock market flotations and rights issues. The individuals and funds that invest within the market are increasingly looking for large, short-term gains. To provide the reward necessary to attract the investment, companies are increasingly forced into allowing dividends which previous orthodoxy would have considered extravagant and recouping their costs by cutting the pay and benefits to their staff. The effect of this is to make the workforce less secure, and this affects their consumption and spending habits in the general market. Consumers are less willing to spend large sums or tie themselves into long-term spending commitments, and as a result the home market for British industry experiences weak and more variable demand. This has all the ingredients of a vicious spiral of decline. The 30/30/40 society rears its ugly head again in the plight of the construction industry, traditionally a solid ally of the Government. Twenty-five-year mortgages were based on the notion of secure jobs; consumer insecurity has produced unstable demand for new housing precisely because consumers are ever more cautious about tying themselves into what could be the biggest financial commitment of their lives.

Then there are the issues surrounding privatisation and the running of the privatised utilities. Fat-cat pay cheques and share option scandals have done little to boost public confidence in the Government's privatisation programme even though Government ministers have called for restraint in Britain's boardrooms. The industry brief also contains all the policy decisions connected to the new technology. We are experiencing an industrial revolution faster and more pervasive than the great industrial boom of the last century; government has a central role to play in the encouragement and regulation of information technology as it permeates our working lives.

Conservatives

Mr Major is fond of recalling his father's past as a garden-ornaments salesman; it gives him an opportunity to identify with the small businesses of Britain, and that is where the main emphasis of Conservative policy development is likely to be placed. But industry in general comes under the Conservatives' banner statement of an enterprise economy, with its ingredients of low tax, low regulation and low public spending. In the Conservatives' view they can effectively contrast their 'hands off' approach to industry with what they denounce as Labour's old-fashioned commitment to regulation and corporatism in New Labour clothes.

Small businesses are seen by the Conservatives as the engine-room of the economic recovery, the sector of industry that will create more jobs faster and will increase their share of the market as they grow. But for the Conservatives small businesses also have a social value as the embodiment of what Major calls 'the society of opportunity', where individuals are able to take responsibility for themselves, take risks, work hard and reap the reward, almost a more restrained and tasteful British version of the American dream. Such a society is made up of people who also take responsibility for their own families and their employees and that must prove attractive to any government seeking to cut the welfare budget.

The Conservatives have applauded the fact that small businesses have created a total of two million jobs over the last fifteen years, but setting up a small firm is still full of risks and uncertainties. In the late 1980s it was pointed out that 50 per cent failed in their first year. In 1994, 450,000 were set up but 390,000 folded. Small businessmen are just as likely as the chiefs of industry to be concerned about the prospects for the business environment. In 1995 an NOP survey of the sector found that 33 per cent of those surveyed were less confident of the prospects for the economy than they were in January of the same year. Among small business experts such as bankers, accountants and financial advisers confidence showed a similar fall: only 31 per cent were more confident about the state of the economy compared to 52 per cent in September 1994. Meanwhile Britain's trade deficit in 1995 with countries outside the European Union was its highest for three years. Against this backdrop the Conservatives are keen to help the small firms over the problems that so many of them face in their first few years of existence.

Major is committed to launching a massive consultation exercise around the country in the run-up to the next election. The consultation will take the form of eleven regional seminars at which local businesses can suggest ways in which the Conservatives can help. The results will be drawn together at a national conference in London and will form a part of a new competitiveness White Paper to be launched in the summer of 1996. The Conservatives hope that their emphasis on cutting red tape will steady those businessmen who have been drifting away in their political support and mark out a practical approach to helping small businesses. The Prime Minister has said that reducing the administrative burden of regulations on VAT, Pay As You Earn and National Insurance contributions will be a priority. The party claims to have taken 100,000 small firms out of the VAT net by raising the threshold during this last government. They will also be concentrating their fire on Labour support for a minimum wage and the social chapter, alleging that both of these would raise costs for small businesses.

Labour

The Labour Party has been cuddling up to the bosses. That's the message of the charm offensive launched by Gordon Brown and Tony Blair in the boardrooms of British industry and the City. The Labour leadership projects itself as just as full of economic rectitude as the Tories, but with a fresh commitment to new ideas and providing more of a 'hands on' boost for the industrial sector. There will be large areas of continuity between present government industrial policy and the actions of any new Labour government. Policies to help small businesses, for example, such as the Business Links Initiative, are likely to be continued, developed and expanded. In matters of industrial policy Labour has first to allay the fears of what a new socialist government might do and then convince businessmen that its agenda adds up and can be implemented.

On the charm offensive things are going Labour's way. The reaction from the CBI adopts a tone of surprised warmth: Labour's call for increased business investment 'is not out of line with our own thinking'. Brown's proposal for a two-tier capital gains tax to encourage longer-term holdings of assets is 'lifted from our Budget proposals last year, which we welcome'. They also look kindly on Labour's proposal to double tax allowances for additional plant and machinery as a short-term boost for the manufacturing sector. The battle has not yet been won. Labour's plans to reduce the burden of VAT on small firms, which echo those of the Conservatives, bring a cautious response with the CBI arguing that this could give small businesses a competitive edge which would be unfair. The CBI still objects to Labour's stance on the single currency and the minimum wage, worries about detail on the policies, and in the last resort wonders if a Labour government can deliver under stress, but relations have never before been so good between the party and the representatives of British industry.

Meanwhile Blair has joined Major on the consultation circuit, setting up a range of meetings across the country to hear the views of businessmen, there will be a special conference bringing together industrialists, academics and politicians to flesh out the idea of the stakeholder economy and Labour has established a series of forums, groups of industrialists and businessmen who are prepared to help work through the policy problems with Labour spokesmen. Blair has also attempted to demonstrate his appeal to foreign businessmen and his ability to 'bat for Britain' in overseas markets. During his tour of the Far East, where he launched the idea of the stakeholder economy, he made a point of emphasising the attractions of investing in Britain: the presence of a skilled, well-educated and adaptable workforce, the access to European markets and the benefits of the English language for the business environment. This was heady stuff, reminiscent of any Tory minister on the hunt for overseas contracts were it not for the emphasis on social cohesion and the role of social policy in providing a secure background for business to operate against. Intriguingly this will have appealed to his audience, for the Asian economies rely on social cohesion for a stable workforce in a way rarely appreciated by recent ministerial tours.

Two of Labour's most radical proposals have, however, caused more trouble at home. In the first, a bid to encourage the better development of the technological infrastructure, Blair has come to an agreement with British Telecom: the prohibition preventing them from competing against the cable companies for franchises to cable up the country would be broken in return for the opportunity to connect British schools, libraries and hospitals to the information superhighway without charge. The details of this are vague. As Labour came under fire for the proposal so the party began to clam up. Labour dismissed Conservative allegations that this amounted to a background deal and said instead that an 'understanding' had been reached. Blair's office refused to release the correspondence in which the details had been set out on the grounds that the letters were 'highly confidential'.

In opting for such an agreement Labour has some strong reasons in support of its case. The policy echoes the recommendations of the all-party Trade and Industry Select Committee which said that both BT and Mercury should be allowed to compete with the cable providers. There is an obvious public benefit in securing connections in an area of current under-investment. At present fewer than 10 per cent of libraries are connected to the superhighway. However, the policy has come under attack from the Government, the Independent Television Commission and the Treasury. They argue that allowing BT into the market could put at risk deals already struck with the cable companies and jeopardise millions of pounds of revenue from the licence fees that the Treasury already expects to receive; it is estimated that several hundred millions of pounds could be at stake. For example, Cable Tel, an American company, bid 14.5 million for the right to cable Northern Ireland and expects to pay the Treasury a percentage of its revenue for the first five years of operation. In 1999 many of the original operating licences come up for renewal and the sums could get larger with the ITC deciding a fair price for each licence; that price will be affected by BT's presence in the market. The Conservatives have claimed that the deal is impossible because it would require changes to BT's licensing conditions.

More controversially Labour has said that it will impose a one-off 'windfall' tax on the privatised utilities to help fund its battle against unemployment. Labour calls the tax a 'Utilities Monopoly Levy' and has refused to say how much it plans to raise. Most estimates suggest a figure of about 3 billion. Gordon Brown claims that the utilities such as the regional electricity companies (RECS), the water companies and the National Grid are the prime targets, while British Gas and BT will also come under scrutiny. The Labour Party claims, despite denials to the contrary, that not only have the utilities benefited from being under-priced at sale and under-taxed in their first years of operation but they have also been squirrelling away funds to meet the eventuality of such a levy. In Labour's view they can well afford to pay. The tax will allow Labour to raise money for training and unemployment without having to raise personal taxation. The proposed tax has caught the imagination of commentators, and Conservative back-benchers even recommended that Kenneth Clarke should trump Labour by introducing the tax before the next election.

But there have been objections, not least from the utility companies themselves. They claim that any such tax will have to be passed on to customers in the form of higher bills if the industries are to maintain adequate levels of investment in their capital projects and environmental improvements. For the electricity companies, the Electricity Association has said that the RECs already pay £1 billion a year in corporation tax while investing £3 billion a year in capital expenditure, and the water industry claims that it is investing twice as much as it makes in profits. The CBI has attacked the proposal as 'arbitrary and unfair' while loyalist Conservatives have accused Labour of wanting to tax success.

The windfall tax is undeniably popular, and faces the charge of being populist. The utility companies have made themselves into general hate figures with their poor levels of service, price rises and the fat-cat salaries and bonuses for their executives. The Conservatives have not been immune from using this sort of tax in the past; in the early 1980s a Conservative government levied a windfall tax on banks. There has been a trend for companies to avoid paying taxes. It used to be usual for companies to pay 20 to 30 per cent of their profits in tax; in 1992 the proportion was 10.8 per cent for industrial companies and 8 per cent for financial firms. The case with the utilities is worse: the water companies were given a seven-year tax holiday on privatisation, while the electricity companies paid half the amount in tax that their publicly owned predecessors had paid in the same period prior to privatisation.

Labour is also open to charges of a return to the politics of envy and of penalising success and enterprise. Many critics denounce the scheme as a breach of contract, the unilateral and retrospective changing of the terms of the agreement under which the firms were privatised. There is also a chance that the companies might retaliate in the run-up to the election by off-loading funds that they have used to bolster their share price and maintain shareholder loyalty. This would mean that the tax would bite not into fat but into flesh, and would result in reductions in staffing and a fall in the level of service offered to the public. Finally there is some doubt as to whether or not such a tax would even have the desired effect. The Institute for Fiscal Studies (IFS) has queried Brown's assumption that £1.5 billion raised in this way will cure youth unemployment and pay for itself in increased tax receipts and falls in benefits expenditure. The tax is not repeatable or it cannot be regarded as a windfall, and according to the Institute any increase in tax revenues will be needed to cut borrowing. The IFS also points out that the victims of the tax are likely to be current shareholders rather than those who bought the shares at rock-bottom prices on privatisation. Utility shares prove particularly popular with the small-scale investor because of their reputation for security. Labour could end up hurting the very people it professes to want to help.

Liberal Democrats

The Liberal Democrats agree with the major parties on the need to maintain investment in industry, a stable economy and improvements in the skills of the workforce, but having agreed on the basics they part company from Labour and Conservative. The Liberal Democrats advocate far greater control and regulation with the creation of new structures to oversee industry and the setting of more limits and regulations on individual business sectors.

They point to the steady destruction of Britain's manufacturing base, where nearly a third of the industry has vanished over the last sixteen years of Conservative rule, as an example of the lack of a co-ordinated approach to industry. This is not entirely fair; a worldwide recession had a fair amount to do with the collapse of the manufacturing industry. The Liberal Democrats, like Labour, are committed to joining the single currency and signing up for the social chapter.

On business itself, the Liberal Democrats lump together both small and medium-sized businesses. They identify the main problem as a need to find better sources of funding to ensure that these businesses get off the ground and do not collapse at the current rate. Policy proposals include co-operating with the banks to establish new sources of finance and in particular equity finance. They would also invest in developing Mutual Guarantee Schemes. They would legislate to allow interest to be charged on the late payment of debt and make it obligatory for companies to publish the amount they spend on such interest. This attacks a perennial problem for small companies where the late payment of invoices causes cash flow problems and the inability to meet their own bills, which can often contribute to the company going out of business. They would also oblige banks to inform their customers of any changes in bank charges, a particular worry for new companies that have borrowed money to set up. As a party with their main strength in local government, they are pledged to reform the Uniform Business Rate, directing the funds entirely to local authorities who will be given greater discretion to discriminate in favour of small businesses. This may provoke howls of protest from other companies maintaining that there will not then be a level playing-field, but the Liberal Democrats would argue that the small and medium business sector is so crucial to the economy that such favouritism is justified.

As a party committed to a strong regional policy, the Liberal Democrats are keen to let new Regional Development Agencies take over and rationalise many of the functions currently exercised by separate offices such as the Government's regional offices, the regional technology centres and the liaison programmes with universities and colleges. Regional Development Agencies would be given a new pool for 'seed corn' funding to help get new businesses off the ground. The Liberal Democrats also want to see the banks establish regional investment branches for local input, although the banks will probably maintain that their current system of regional offices already performs this function.

The Liberal Democrats are very much the party of the new technologies, with a strong representation in the party leadership from the southern IT triangle stretching from London to Bath.

The party has concentrated its fire on what it perceives as the serious danger that Britain will fall behind its competitors if it does not take the challenge of the computer age seriously. It promises a substantial injection of funds into the science budget, amounting to at least 0.4 per cent of GDP each year. To direct its IT strategy it would create a new Cabinet Committee chaired by a Liberal Democrat Prime Minister to raise science and technology up the political priority list.

The Liberal Democrats are not above a little pork-barrel politics in response to the initiatives of the major parties. At the time of the last Budget, with Labour advocating a windfall tax and Kenneth Clarke being encouraged from his own back benches to do the same, the Liberal Democrats advocated a 'Rip-Off Rebate' under which each of the utility companies' twenty-two million consumers would receive a one-off £130 rebate to compensate them for the huge profits made by the utilities since privatisation. This was populist politics at its best and was backed up by little argument and not really taken seriously by commentators at the time. It remains to be seen if this pledge will make it into the manifesto.

There are other proposals to regulate the utilities that make more sense. They would impose a new pricing policy on utilities related to the expected rate of return so that services which involve little or no risk to the provider would be charged at a lower rate to the customer. They would cut down on the profits made for shareholders by passing profits, probably in the form of price cuts, on to the consumer. They would require public hearings with the opportunity for consumers to give evidence whenever the utilities want to raise their prices. The water companies would be prohibited from cutting customers off for non-payment of bills. The energy utilities and industries would be subject to a nationally imposed energy strategy under a pan-European energy policy, and the party would break up British Telecom into its component parts and stop the privatisation of the Post Office.

Summary

There is general agreement on the part of all parties that small businesses are a key to the industrial sector. It is certainly true that abolishing red tape would help the workload of many small businesses, but any judgment on Conservative and Labour policy in this area will have to await the results of their separate exercises in consulting around the country. These consultations may well produce dividends. It is always important for the parties to keep in close touch with the people their policies affect, but at the same time such consultation should be a continuous process from one election to the next. These special meetings in the last year before an election smack more of a publicity stunt than a serious exercise. One wonders how either party can operate on a Finance Bill, the annual major piece of legislation affecting business costs, if they do not know what business wants in this area and have no firm plans for how they would like to help small businesses. Liberal Democrat policy with its detail scores well here, but it is subject to the charge that it is just too Utopian and each voter will have to assess the party's ability to deliver. Moreover, such an interventionist strategy is not the current fashion in politics and not for those voters who take the free-market line.

The rows about Labour's utility windfall tax and the deal with British Telecom may prove an Achilles' heel for the party, particularly in its struggle to convince the business community of its reformed character. Setting aside the questions of cost and effectiveness, many in the City will regard this as an old example of the politics of envy, and what is more as a breach of contract, with Labour unilaterally and retrospectively altering the terms of the privatisation agreement long after the ink has dried. If it can do this to the utilities, why not to other industrial sectors if it needs the money? Labour will have to prove that the utilities are a special case, dealt with on special terms, and its argument will be carefully scrutinised.

On the other hand there is a strong case for arguing that companies in their search for short-term profit and their lax tax treatment should be contributing more to the national funds. No one party has produced a credible strategy for tackling this basic flaw at the heart of British business. Whether any can do this by the election remains to be seen.

Rural affairs

Britain's countryside and the environment in which we live are part of our national heritage, and yet both are under threat. The urbanisation of society brought about by the rush of population to the towns to fuel the factories of the industrial revolution changed for ever the nature of rural England. Other factors such as agricultural developments and war (half the land in England changed hands after the slaughter in the trenches of the First World War) have also contributed to a changing countryside. Now we face a second and perhaps more profound revolution for rural Britain. The technological revolution is working itself out not so much in industrialisation as suburbanisation, as more and more of our rural communities become dormitories for commuters or weekend retreats for the wealthy city-worker. There was once a hope that the computer age would provide the population with more leisure time to enjoy the rural heritage, but such hopes have been largely unfounded. Increasing technology has been more likely to increase working hours as workers are expected to cope with higher and higher burdens with the aid of their computers and faxes. The leisure that has been created is largely enforced, and the unemployed are not going to boost the economy of rural England.

As the rural economy has changed so the pressures on life and work within the rural environment have changed. There has always been a tendency to regard the countryside as little more than an open-air museum, a recreational resource to be preserved in picturesque aspic for the benefit of tourists and weekend residents. This attitude is neither practical nor desirable. It is also historically inaccurate. The rural environment we regard as natural, whether in the Lakes or the South West, is the product of centuries of man's impact on the environment. The moors of northern England are romantically desolate and treeless due to the activity of the humble sheep. Like any society and economy rural England is in a constant process of change, and treating farmers and villagers as merely museum exhibits is hardly fair. Not that tourism is irrelevant; it remains a big money-earner for rural communities and provides the opportunity for hard-pressed farms and villages to diversify into new forms of employment and earning. Nor is it desirable for the countryside to be a free-marketeer's Mecca, subject to the whims of deregulation and cut-throat finance. The laws of the free market are no respecters of heritage and have no appreciation for Sites of Special Scientific Interest or the preservation of rare forms of orchid.

As in other areas, a policy for our rural environment must strike a balance, in this case between the needs of the people who live and work there and society's demands for a rural playground. Agriculture is very much an industry and we all depend on it. It is an industry in crisis, with general complaints about the operation of the Common Agricultural Policy and the level and purpose of agricultural subsidies. As rural industry is in crisis so rural communities are equally under pressure. Villages are dying on their feet and the last few decades have seen a steady erosion of community facilities, from village schools to post offices, in the name of greater efficiency.

Since 1945 the numbers employed in agriculture have fallen from more than a million, including 700,000 farm labourers, to 430,000, of whom only 200,000 are labourers. (Other industries apart from agriculture have also been badly hit. The numbers employed by rural collieries have fallen over the past ten years from 60,000 to 5,500.) Agriculture is no longer the major employer that it was. Although farms take up a massive 77 per cent of the landscape they employ no more than 1.3 per cent of the workforce. The highest share of the workforce employed in farming, even in the most remote rural areas, is no more than 10 per cent.

On the continent this scale of job-shedding in agriculture has led to massive depopulation. Not in Britain. Instead we have a net influx of population moving into the countryside. The numbers living in rural England have risen by more than 17 per cent since 1971, increasing from 11.1 million to 12.9 million, but those living in the countryside account for only a quarter of the population. Many of those living in rural communities are not classified as economically active. There are those seeking the good life after retirement, and the commuters and weekenders who tend to under-use the village shops and services on which so much rural employment depends. But the influx has also brought new employment opportunities, with 1.2 million manufacturing jobs (equalling 31 per cent of Britain's depleted manufacturing sector) now located in the countryside, and 3.5 million service sector jobs, equivalent to 25 per cent of the total, situated in rural areas.

The extent of the countryside is also under pressure with new building, roads and developments encroaching on the rural environment. Pressure groups and government bodies such as the Council for the Protection of Rural England and the Countryside Commission have warned of the shrinking nature of the countryside and the impact of greater access in destroying wilderness areas. Those who live in the country have always maintained that those who decide policy or lobby for change are city dwellers with little understanding for the problems they face. There is no greater example of the difference in views between town and country than the heated dispute over hunting and field sports. Those who defend such activities point out that they are a crucial factor in the preservation of the economy with habitats maintained to safeguard the sport; for example, the popularity of fishing has meant a constant pressure to ensure the cleanliness of streams and rivers. Field sports also make a major contribution to the rural economy, generating in excess of £2.7 billion a year and providing much employment.

There are deep emotions involved in both the electors' and the politicians' reactions to the problems of the rural environment. Rural Britain is a central part of our cultural heritage, and the policies we adopt for its preservation and development will be crucial to whether we pass on to future generations a lifeless and desecrated playground or a living and vibrant resource for all.

Conservatives

The Conservatives have always felt that they have a special relationship with the countryside. The more romantically inclined like to dwell on the party's origins among the landed gentry and enthuse about a golden rural past of mutual obligations and patronage. Such Conservatives tend to inhabit the One Nation part of the party; the new Thatcherite right have no such emotional link to the countryside.

It used to be taken for granted that farmers voted Conservative. Nothing could be further from the truth today. The times when agricultural labourers could lose their jobs and housing for supporting the wrong party are long gone, as are the agricultural sector's ties to the Tories. Nowadays it is impossible to generalise about the reaction of the industry to political parties, except to say that across agriculture growing concerns, insecurity and falling incomes are making the farmers a more critical audience of the proposals of any political party. But they are no longer the central audience in any rural seat and the fall in the numbers of people employed in the sector has marginalised much of their voting power. There is also a big difference between, for example, small fifty-acre upland farms struggling to survive and the big lowland estates on the prairies of East Anglia. Each has its own concerns and its own priorities. Even the large landowners are expressing reservations. In the autumn of 1995 Ewen Cameron, the Deputy President of the Country Landowners' Association, warned the Government that it could not count on the support of the members of the Association. All of which is rather unfair for the Secretary of State for the Environment, John Gummer, who has proved an energetic minister widely respected for his commitment to the rural environment.

The heart of Conservative policy for the countryside which will form the basis for any pledges in the manifesto has been set out in the Government's White Paper *Rural England, a nation committed to a living countryside*, published in October 1995, and the first comprehensive attempt to make proposals by any government for half a century. In its analysis and recommendations the Conservatives have attempted to produce a complete policy package for the rural environment linked into general policy umbrellas such as the Citizens' Charter and the Enterprise Economy. For example, the government promises a 'Rural Charter' to improve services and breathe new life into rural communities.

With regard to rural planning the government aims to cut red tape and encourage the better and more diverse use of rural land. A new 'good practice guide' will be produced for local authorities to boost development and rural businesses with a follow-up circular encouraging planning appeals to be processed faster than at present. A new 'Rural Business Use' class is being considered to allow local authorities to encourage diversification, but it is also proposed that there should be limits applied to the new class to ensure that it does not generate large amounts of traffic and the threat of uncontrolled expansion. The Conservatives are also seeking to persuade councils to discriminate in favour of allowing disused rural buildings to be converted for business use rather than as dwellings, many of which would be beyond the pockets of many of the rural community. The planning recommendations also seek to encourage the use of local materials in building projects to ensure that new buildings and renovations are in keeping with regional styles.

On housing, the Government plans to exempt villages with fewer than 3,000 inhabitants from the provisions of the right-to-buy scheme. This proposal is a U-turn from previous government policy which encouraged right-to-buy schemes but which many rural pressure groups condemned as pricing homes out of local reach and encouraging those who, living in the country but working in the city, can afford higher house prices. The Government hopes that this proposal will encourage landowners to provide more land for development. The government itself will be setting an example by concentrating new house building as far as possible on surplus land owned by the Ministry of Defence rather than in greenfield sites. At the same time Gummer is on the record as being committed to look first to decaying inner-city areas for land for new housing rather than destroying yet more green belt land.

On farming, many of the proposals depend on reform of the Common Agricultural Policy. While there is much support for reform of some kind in a policy that takes the lion's share of the European Union's budget, there is no appetite for urgent reform. Some savings on subsidy prices could be available to plough back into the rural environment if reform is forthcoming. Meanwhile the Conservatives are likely to concentrate on expanding the 'Countryside Stewardship Scheme' whereby farmers outside environmentally sensitive areas are paid to use environmentally sound techniques which protect wildlife. The proposals have a definite green tinge, with more green conditions attached to receipt of subsidies and a proposal to establish a forum combining the government with rural agencies such as English Nature to monitor the expanding green farming schemes and inform government thinking on land management. The Government is committed to encouraging forestry, with the hope that the amount of the countryside covered with economically managed forests will double.

The White Paper proposals also seek to tackle the decline of village communities. Village shops and post offices may get a new form of rates relief. The criteria for the scheme will require parliamentary legislation, but meanwhile local authorities will be urged to examine the wisdom of granting planning permission to new developments that undercut the prices of village shops. There is a recognition as well of the value of village schools, many of them with higher standards than their counterparts in urban areas. The Conservatives are pledged not to allow any future closures of schools except where equally good educational standards are available elsewhere, with factors such as the length of journeys also taken into account. Rural crime will be targeted with 'village watch' schemes. Parish councils may be given, after consultation, much of the power of local authorities in combating crime. They could be allowed to approve the installation of closed circuit television monitors and will be encouraged to take the major role in the recruiting, training and management of special constables.

On transport, the Conservatives are committed to improving the motorways and taking the pressure of road development off rural areas. This will mean more town and village by-passes. For the villagers themselves the Conservatives set great store in the parish councils, whom they want to see take responsibility for local transport. Under a Conservative government parish councils would be encouraged to survey the transport needs of their communities, to set up taxi and car-sharing schemes for the most needy members of the community, and to launch community mini-bus services to replace the network of rural bus services which have all but disappeared. The Conservatives want to encourage local volunteers to take over local railway services and local authorities to be more imaginative in their approach to the alternative transport usage of disused railway lines as cycle routes, footpaths and bridleways.

Criticism of the Conservative proposals for the countryside centres on the fact that they appear long on detail and encouragement but short on the means and timetable to achieve their objectives. Many of the proposals are far from new; of those that affect local government, most would be considered current good practice and are being implemented at present. There is little or no extra money on offer to implement these proposals, the Department of the Environment being subject to just the same financial pressures as the rest of government. This is also one of the reasons why the Conservatives have rejected the proposal of the Country Landowners' Association to set up a new Department of Rural Affairs and have opted instead for a Cabinet Committee expanding its role from the environment to encompass countryside issues. Given little money the Government is forced to rely on the voluntary efforts of local people active in their parish councils. There are many who would say that this is one of the main strengths of the package. All too often, provision of services by faceless bodies higher up the administrative tree has killed off volunteer and community participation. A commitment to local services provided where possible by local people would be therefore very welcome. However, those who are keen to boost local voluntary efforts would be wary of a policy package designed only to save money and lacking the philosophical commitment to interdependent villages and rural communities.

Labour

The Labour Party has traditionally been seen, and has seen itself, as a metropolitan party, representing the interests of the workers in the industrial heartlands of the country. This industrial vision of Labour was not without exceptions – the coal industry, among others, once had a significant rural presence – but hardly enough to destroy the general image of a party of the cities and suburbs.

Electoral realities are changing that image and Labour needs to pay more attention to the rural vote than ever before. Labour did well in many rural areas in the European elections of 1994 and in the 1995 council elections, for example gaining control of Bedfordshire, and is likely to make ground again when the shire elections are held before the general election. From Scotland to the South Labour now has seats traditionally thought of as safe for the Tories within its sights. In Scotland constituencies such as Stirling have large rural hinterlands. In England Derbyshire South and Erewash are both Labour targets. All this means that those who live in the countryside have not been immune from Tony Blair's charm offensive. The Labour leader is even known to don green wellies when he tours farms. But rural affairs have never been high on the party's priority lists and remain a junior shadow minister's responsibility. Tony Blair has restricted his comments on the countryside to a general sketch of principles and a traditional swipe at his political enemies. Blair claims that Labour understands that the countryside is not a 'theme park' and promises to make the Labour Party a 'party of the countryside, of rural as well as urban areas'.

The policy detail is sketchy but the form of manifesto commitments is beginning to take shape. Labour is committed to reform of the Common Agricultural Policy, pledged to negotiate the end of 'wasteful price support of surplus produce'. Labour wants to see an end to the massive amounts of agricultural fraud in the European Union and wants to replace subsidies with new incentives to diversify land use and encourage social and environmentally responsible land use. Labour does not say how it plans to achieve this and if it gains government is likely to find itself facing the same lack of enthusiasm on the continent for CAP reform as the Conservatives.

But Labour is wise enough not to limit its rural interests to agriculture and is well apprised of the importance of manufacturing and service sector jobs to the rural economy. Blair argues that information technology, in particular the information super highway, has the capacity to transform employment opportunities in rural areas. Labour's anti-Conservative rhetoric blames the past government for the decline in rural bus services, shops and post offices and argues that the Conservatives have not done enough to reduce unemployment in rural areas.

Labour has pledged that it will expand the responsibilities of the Ministry for Agriculture, returning to it the responsibility for food under a new junior minister. This might please farmers and consumers, but Blair has also retreated from traditional Labour positions, such as by assuring rural voters that Labour will not allow a 'right to roam' over the countryside, and that it will consult first with landowners and the pressure groups before setting out on any large capital expenditure. Such noises have produced a welcome response from those organisations working in rural affairs. That traditional friend of the Conservatives, the Country Landowners' Association, has commented on the degree of ideas it holds in common with New Labour. Its appreciation began to soar after Labour did away with Clause 4, which pledged any future Labour government to nationalise land-holdings. In the words of the Deputy President of the Association: 'We can work with New Labour.'

Liberal Democrats

The Liberal Democrats have always had close contact with the rural vote. Even at the nadir of their fortunes it was rural support that kept the old Liberal Party alive on the Celtic fringe of Devon and Cornwall, Wales and the Highlands and Islands. The Liberal Democrats have built on this tradition and now form the leading opposition to the Conservatives across swathes of rural Britain, particularly in the South West. The

Liberal Party has traditionally been the preferred voting choice of small farmers and the small firms of the countryside. The new Liberal Democrats while inheriting this resource, have added other green and 'ecologically sound' support which has been an increasing group in the rural population, again particularly in the South West.

The Liberal Democrats have a strong local feel to their policies, as befits a party with a strong local base and a tradition of community politics. Liberal Democrats in rural seats spend their lives defending local post offices and drawing up petitions and running campaigns in support of threatened schools. Generally they agree with the consensus of the problems for the rural environment and home in on the Common Agricultural Policy as a major source of conflict, but their policy pledges are among the greenest in British politics, with a strong emphasis on the revitalisation of the rural economy through the application of the new technologies.

On the Common Agricultural Policy, the Liberal Democrats want to see this replaced by what they call the 'Common Rural Policy'. In this replacement, agriculture plays a role, but not an exclusive one. The Liberal Democrats want to concentrate funds as well on start-up costs for small businesses and help to agriculture to diversify away from over-production. Under this scheme subsidies are targeted on social needs rather than maintaining the income of farmers and by extension encouraging over-production. The party hopes that this will wipe out the problem of surpluses and encourage European farmers to be competitive on a world market basis. The Common Rural Policy is good in principle but extremely difficult to achieve in practice. The Liberal Democrats are advocating a more radical reform than that of the other two parties; if they are going to face problems negotiating such a deal through Europe, the Liberal Democrats will face even more.

On general agricultural policy, the Liberal Democrats are committed to supporting measures that would be of most benefit to the small farms sector. They would encourage produce to be processed locally, ensuring that the local trade would benefit the local community. They favour the forming of marketing co-operatives and joint ventures between food producers and the commercial sector, and they place considerable importance on maintaining the tenanted farm sector as a first step on the ladder for aspiring farmers and as a system that encourages small family farms.

The second major plank of Liberal Democrat policy is the intro-duction of what they call 'Countryside Management Contracts'. The emphasis of such contracts is almost entirely environmental. Under them, green farming methods that conserve and maintain wildlife habitats would be encouraged. Under this system farmers would be able to choose options from a regionally set menu of contracts. Each item would be worth a number of points which would translate into money claimable from a local fund. This is an imaginative scheme which would allow regional environmental policies to be determined together with incentives to encourage take-up. The snag is finding the money for the funds, and the Liberal Democrats have not said whether these will be funds separate from the Common Rural Policy or dependent on its renegotiation. The party is also pledged to reforming the planning system in favour of greener criteria and to encouraging public access to the countryside, but balanced against the rights of those who live in rural communities.

For the rural economy outside agriculture, the Liberal Demo-crats place a great emphasis on encouraging distance working through the use of information technology. They envisage what they have charmingly called 'telecottages' where people who once would have commuted to work are enabled to live in the countryside through IT links. They agree with the Conservatives on the need to double the area of land under forestry but in addition they are committed to reforming the taxation and grant systems for commercial forests.

For local communities, the Liberal Democrats offer a strategy which they say aims at a basic level of provision to rural villages. They would increase the presence of the police and deter crime by stationing more policemen in towns and large villages, encourage local councils to draw up community transport strategies and plans, ensure that a mix of housing types be built to allow all income groups to live in the countryside, and provide more funds for village schools, increasing their community use and using IT to link them into wider educational networks. They would exempt village post offices from the business rates and expand the services they offer to make them more viable.

At the governmental level the Liberal Democrats would indulge in a large-scale bout of reorganisation. There would be a new Department for Natural Resources, absorbing most of the responsibilities of the current Ministry of Agriculture but with further responsibility for rural economic, environmental and social policy. There would be a new Rural Policy Unit at the Cabinet Office and their new national Parliaments and regional assemblies in England would set the terms of the countryside management contracts.

Summary

There is perhaps more unanimity on rural policy than in many other areas of the political debate. All the major parties put reform of the Common Agricultural Policy at the top of their political agendas. At present it is probably also the most unachievable policy promise. The detail of rural policy also produces a broad range of agreement; all the parties are pledged to review the local business rates, to attempt to reverse the decline in village shops and schools and to encourage more environmentally sustainable patterns of agriculture and diversification.

Labour's policy is marked out by its sketchiness. The party will have to do some serious work to present any credible policy programme by the time of the election. This has not stopped Labour becoming a more popular option in the countryside as support for the Tories declines and Labour begins to increase its rural profile.

The Conservative policy package is characterised by its emphasis on the development of village voluntaryism centred on an expanded role for parish councils. This makes good democratic sense and could provide a massive strengthening of community bonds; however, electors will need to assess whether the support will be there to ease parish councils into their new role. Past Conservative governments are littered with plans such as the Care in the Community Programme and the Child Support

Agency where everyone applauded the principle but where the policy failed for lack of resources.

It remains to be seen whether or not the policies on offer from all the parties can be properly funded. In the past the countryside has suffered from a lack of interest and a lack of public funds to support essential community services. All sides now agree that such services need central support and subsidy to be maintained. Can they put our money where their mouths are?

Health

There's no consensus on the state of the National Health Service. Underlying the debate is a persistent current of unease, a feeling that a system, once the pride of our Welfare State, is running out of control and unable to meet the demands that we make on it. In a recent speech to the annual conference of the NHS Trusts Federation, Roy Lilley, the former Chairman of the Homewood Trust and a pioneer of health service reforms, said that the NHS would collapse within a decade, doomed by its inability to fund increasingly costly treatments and escalating demands. He blamed the politicians, who he said were unwilling to take the unpopular decisions necessary to maintain the service, and accused the NHS of sacrificing quality in the pursuit of greater throughput. His remarks were described as 'drive' by Philip Hunt, Director of the National Association of Health Authorities and Trusts, who claimed that the NHS was one of the most robust health-care systems in the world. Meanwhile Rodney Walker, an outgoing Chairman of the NHS Trusts Federation, has claimed that the future of universal provision of free hospital treatment is under threat from the growing demands on the service; his comments were contradicted by the then Health Secretary, Peter Lilley. Sir Duncan Nichol, the former Chief Executive of the NHS, has pointed out that the gap between demand and provision is unlikely to close without a radical rethink. As Chairman of Healthcare 2000, he has called for the prioritisation of treatments and the increased use of private care. A survey by the National Association of Health Authorities and Trusts in 1995 revealed that 11 out of 66 health authorities were now rationing non-essential treatments, up from 4 in the previous year, while in general practice, the NHS's front line, there is now an increasing shortage of trainee doctors, with up to half the training vacancies unfilled in some parts of the country.

For the general public, the sight of health service experts quarrelling over the state of the NHS is far from reassuring. Combined with persistent reports of the lack of beds and patients being shuttled massive distances for treatment, it comes as no surprise that opinion polls show great concern for the future of the NHS. There is a persistent fear that the NHS is turning into a two-tier system, with excellent provision for those who can afford private care or who are fortunate enough to be serviced by general practices with a strong funding base, and a more inadequate, rationed, emergency-concentrated arrangement for those depending on free health care. Moreover, evidence for the existence of the demographic time bomb is incontrovertible. The proportion of the population over eighty-five years old is expected to increase from 2 per cent to 5 per cent by 2050. According to the research group London Economics, this means that the cost of long-term care will rise from £12 billion to £34.5 billion by 2030, while the direct costs to the tax payer will increase from £7.2 billion to £16 billion. If current trends continue private provision is unlikely to save the day. Most people in Britain expect to be provided for in their old age by the NHS and their National Insurance contributions. The latter will have been spent long ago. Improvident governments have been spending National Insurance receipts; no fund has been built up to carry the cost. At present only 18 per cent of the population expect to contribute financially to their care in old age. However, it is not too late for the politicians to get a grip on the problem. Britain still has a relatively young population compared to the rest of Europe. At present in Germany each worker is expected to contribute a sum equivalent to 1 per cent of their annual earnings to a new national fund to care for the elderly; such a system is currently thought by the civil servants to be unnecessary in Britain.

The NHS has gone through massive change in the last decade. The establishment of Health Trusts to manage hospitals, the creation of an internal market and the introduction of GP contracts have all been controversial, and the new regime is still under strong criticism for increasing red tape, wasting resources in paying a new managerial elite and the accusation that care has been sacrificed in the name of cost. The issues that lie at the heart of the political debate concern the actions that government can take to improve the system in the face of demands for greater reliance on private provision, and the rationing and cost benefit analysis of the treatments on offer. Some of the proposals currently doing the rounds include charging patients the full cost of their prescriptions (from the right-wing Institute of Economic Affairs), rationing non-essential treatments, expanding private medicine to subsidise free health care and cutting back the number of hospitals to concentrate on regional centres of excellence. The question for the politicians, given the widely divergent views, is: can any party claim that the future of the NHS is safe in its hands?

Conservatives

The Conservatives have been consistently portrayed by the left in British politics as uncommitted to the NHS. Throughout the last sixteen years the Government has faced accusations that it has subjected the NHS to the full force of the market, that it is cutting health costs and moving provision more and more towards a two-tier system. In its defence the Government can claim that it has tackled the worst excesses of a service where costs and wastage were running out of control and that it has put in place radical reforms to ensure that a universal service continues at the best possible cost to the country. But health policy has seen considerable changes in government and Health Secretaries have been firmly in the firing line. Virginia Bottomley pursued policies based on the orthodoxies of the past two decades; she concentrated on developing a smaller number of hospitals which were destined to be regional centres of excellence. As a result a total of 245 hospitals have been closed since 1990 and a further 86 are still threatened. Commentators have claimed that this has also reduced the numbers of beds available, with a third of all hospital beds lost since 1985. Public anger at the closure of leading hospitals such as St Bartholomew's in London nearly cost Mrs Bottomley her job. The normal reaction of Conservative ministers in the firing line on health policy has been to counter with a barrage of statistics deployed to show that government spending on the NHS has been more than generous and that the service is now carrying out more treatments and processing more patients than ever before. Expect to see a selection of such figures in the manifesto. John Major has already promised an extra £5 billion over the five years after a Conservative win at the election.

There has been a change since Stephen Dorrell took over as Secretary of State for Health. In part this has been due to the Conservative leadership election of 1995. John Redwood set out an agenda for health that put increased emphasis on the role of the smaller hospitals and this was welcomed on the back benches as an electorally popular policy. Dorrell, while insisting that he would not revisit the decisions of his predecessors, has responded; cottage hospitals now feature prominently in the Government's proposals for the health service. But at the heart of current Conservative thinking on health policy is the need to tackle the demographic time bomb and keep costs firmly under control. With predictions that 4 out of 9 people in Britain will be either too old or too young to work by the year 2030, the Government is currently engaged in a policy development process to cut back the costs of the Welfare State, and some of the initiatives can be expected to be unveiled in the manifesto. The Conservatives will be seeking to bring about 'a change in culture' by encouraging a greater proportion of the population to make their own provision for health care at an early stage in their working lives. The Conservatives are considering introducing a wider range of tax incentives to persuade people to insure against sickness, and tax relief on long-term savings earmarked for retirement care. The Government hopes that increased private provision combined with the success of the NHS in attracting private patients will take some of the pressures off public funds. Trust hospitals are currently expanding the numbers of private beds; in 1993/4 such hospitals received over £115 million in private fees, money which hospital administrators insist is being used to improve services for NHS patients. At the same time the amount being spent by private patients rose as did the subscriptions to the medical insurance companies. All this will be seen as good news by the Government.

The Government is realistic about the strains on the NHS, and Dorrell has publicly accepted that the growing costs of the NHS will only be affordable if treatments of marginal benefit are given a much lower priority. More research is being commissioned and studied by the Government on the efficacy of particular treatments and there is an insistence on the setting of realistic targets and health-care priorities. One of these will be the concentration of more resources on GPs and improved primary care. Such provision is cheaper than the services offered by the large regional hospitals and more efficient for the patient, as well as being in line with public demand. The Conservatives also have their eye on a reduction in NHS bureaucracy, which they hope will release more funds for improving services. NHS Trusts will be obliged to publish their full administrative costs, expected to average out at more than 10 per cent of their budgets, and the Government is planning to impose a 5 per cent cut, which should net a saving of £140 million. An Efficiency Scrutiny Group is currently examining ways to cut the burden of paperwork on the hospitals. Under these proposals the NHS could see the loss of a considerable number of administrative posts, but the Conservatives are pledged to replacing them with more clinical staff. It remains to be seen which proposals from the various working groups will be considered palatable enough for the manifesto, but the party remains vulnerable to public concern for the health service.

Labour

New Labour has its problems with policy making for the NHS. The party staged a root and branch opposition to the Conservative health reforms but is now faced with a situation where it is impossible to return to the pre-1979 NHS. It has therefore adopted a pragmatic approach, setting out in a policy document, *Renewing the NHS*, the central features of the policy with which it will go into the general election. Labour remains committed to universal provision of free health care and is determined to resist the drift towards a two-tier system implicit in much of the

Conservative reforms. The challenge for Labour policy makers has been to produce a credible programme which builds on the best features of the current system, keeps a brake on costs and yet delivers the necessary product. In essence Labour is committed to replacing the competitive internal market constructed by the Tories with a co-operative managed market. The party has become reconciled to the role of managers and administrators within the NHS, but is committed to abolishing NHS trusts and GP fundholders while restructuring health authorities into the purchasing agency in co-operation with managers and GPs. This 'managed market' which retains a purchaser–provider split has been broadly welcomed by the health authorities. The party takes a swipe at private medicine, which it regards as less efficient at delivering care than the NHS, by pledging to end tax relief on medical insurance.

These proposals have come under fire from a variety of critics. There has been a general criticism of the lack of detail but also more specific accusations that the package is a regurgitated menu from the 1960s, restoring a situation where everyone has a say in provision but no one is in charge. Andrew Wall, a consultant on NHS management, described it in the *Guardian* as involving 'democratic sentimentality and organisational innocence'. The most controversial element in the proposals has proved to be Labour's commitment to abolish general practice fundholding as the root cause of the development of two-tier care and a deterrent to long-term NHS planning. Labour's shadow Health Secretary, Margaret Beckett, has said that the party wishes to replace fundholding with joint commissioning schemes which she claims have produced similar improvements in patient care. The proposal has been deeply criticised by fundholding GPs who value the freedom to purchase care for their patients at the best price and terms. Faced with the threat from fundholding GPs that they might leave the NHS if this proposal was ever implemented, Labour sought to moderate its line, making warm noises about prior consultation and seeking to ensure that the best elements of the system remained in place. Currently 10,000 GPs control their own budgets and service some ten million patients, equivalent to 41 per cent of the population. From April 1996 this proportion was expected to increase to 50 per cent. As Labour prepares to draw up manifesto proposals it appears likely that it will seek to meet the critics with promises of consultation before implementation. This has led to criticisms that Labour is not yet firm on its own proposals and that there will be a lack of government direction if a Labour government comes to power.

The 1997 manifesto will also include measures to cut NHS bureaucracy by £100 million and transfer the resources to cutting waiting lists. This initiative will be specifically aimed at cutting the waiting time for cancer patients. In addition Labour is looking at a return to the cottage hospital system, particularly for assisting patients to recuperate after major surgery. Labour is also committed to banning tobacco adverts.

Liberal Democrats

There is considerable overlap between Liberal Democrat and Labour policies on health. The Liberal Democrats, like Labour, are resigned to working from the base of the Conservative health reforms and are also committed to maintaining the purchaser–provider split and ending GP fundholding in favour of joint commissioning in the localities. There the similarities end, for the Liberal Democrats have never been as hostile to private provision as Labour and see it as playing a role in any health care system. At the same time the Liberal Democrats set their health proposals within a philosophy of improving the health of the nation. Good preventive care and more healthy lifestyles, they argue, will of themselves reduce spending on the NHS. As a result they are committed to banning tobacco advertising and encouraging health authorities and social services departments to work more closely together. In keeping with a general Liberal Democrat emphasis on freedom of information, the party wants to open up the workings of the health service by abolishing secrecy and making health-care bodies more representative and accountable. They would ban the gagging orders that stop medical staff from revealing details of poor care and management and they would make Trusts publish a list of their prices. All this would be supervised by a new National Inspectorate of Health and Social Care, which would have a wide-ranging brief to oversee the workings of the NHS, promote better standards and guard the interests of patients.

While the Liberal Democrats are committed to retaining a comprehensive service, financed from taxation and available to all on the basis of need, they are far from hopeful that the service can be delivered at a lower cost. Instead they intend to fund their proposals, which include a restoration of free optical and dental check-ups and a review of prescription costs, with the imposition of a 5 to 10p tax on twenty cigarettes and increased taxes on alcohol. In their own words: 'Smoking costs the NHS an estimated £610 million per year; 50 million working days are lost to smoking-related diseases every year. It contributes to asthma and pollution and it kills people.'

Summary

In 1994 John Maples, a former Deputy Chairman of the Conservative Party, said in a memorandum on the next election that the Conservatives' best chance of winning would be 'zero media coverage' of the NHS. Since then the news has reported patients dying on trolleys for lack of beds, waiting lists of more than a million and patients carted around the countryside in the search for an empty bed. While there is agreement in politics on the causes of the problem – a declining workforce, a growth in the numbers of the elderly, increased technology and greater demands – there is little consensus on the solution either within the service or at Westminster. There is an inbuilt disincentive for politicians to develop a comprehensive programme that tackles the issues that lie at the root of concern for the NHS and that is the electoral popularity of the service. We treasure the health service. There is almost unanimous support for the principle of free health care for all, and any change in that principle, such as overt rationing or increasing privatisation, is likely to hit our own pockets.

Against this background the Conservatives are beginning to develop policies that will address the root problems, but relying on greater private provision is unlikely to win them many votes and I doubt that any initiatives in this direction will find their way into the manifesto, although support for the cottage hospitals may help. Labour finds itself in a contradictory position. Unable to commit itself to the spending necessary to transform the service because it would mean an unpopular hike in taxes, it is forced to accept much of the current system and recommend organisational tinkering to remove those features of the NHS to which it is most ideologically opposed. No one could oppose the Liberal Democrats' aim to improve the nation's health, but it is difficult to imagine what more could be achieved than is already being done by the myriad of health information with which we are all bombarded.

Benefits

If there's one thing that politicians agree on it is that we cannot go on paying out more and more in benefits within a system that actively discriminates against those who seek work. Unfortunately there is no consensus on how the tough decisions that need to be taken can be sold to the electorate. Long-term gain in any programme of reform must be set against the short-term pain of introducing any changes. This is particularly true for a government with a small majority. Any change to the social security system risks the possibility of a revolt, either from backbenchers in Parliament or from the electorate in the country. Indeed, in such a situation ministers are more tempted to pour extra money into benefits and the wider Welfare State in the hope of securing re-election. This not only affects the government; at the same time the opposition parties are wary of offering a full-scale overhaul of the system in their manifestos for fear that other parties will not. There is also a firm belief that voters will not accept cutbacks in the Welfare State and that therefore any reform must be by stealth. The current Government has opted for this approach with piecemeal measures such as raising the age for women's retirement, cutting back on the length of time for which unemployment benefit is paid and altering the conditions and payments for other benefits. Such a strategy is a long way from paying any rewards. An example of its ineffectiveness is the situation with incapacity benefit. This was introduced as a replacement for invalidity benefit with much tougher entitlements designed to save the government £410 million as 90,000 claimants failed to qualify under the new rules. Recent figures suggest that savings currently amount to 15 per cent of the expected total.

In general while the growth in social security payments has been slowed they are still rising faster than the economy is growing. The trend is for reliance on benefits to rise while wages fall as a proportion of income. Benefits now account for 14 per cent of the average family's income; thirty years ago it was only 8 per cent, while wages have fallen as a part of income from 76 per cent to 64 per cent. Moreover, many argue that the greatest expenditure in the Welfare State is on providing uneeded money to the wealthy middle classes. They benefit just as much as the poor from access to free health care and free education, and receive child benefit no matter how high their income. There is an increasingly vocal school of thought which questions the wisdom of paying benefits across the board and calls for a concentration of welfare spending on the poor, needy and old.

Our Welfare State is no longer the envy of the world. A recent report on European benefits systems showed that the unemployed receive a worse deal in Britain than in any other of the industrialised states in the European Union. Only in Greece and Ireland do those out of work receive less. In Britain an unemployed person receives roughly half of what they would have received if they had been working. In Germany and Italy they would receive 60 per cent of the working wage, more than 70 per cent in Denmark, Spain and the Netherlands and more than 80 per cent in France, Luxembourg and Portugal. The report also criticised Britain for moving towards more means testing of benefits and increasing the emphasis on private pension provision; both, it says, open employees up to unscrupulous treatment from employers and hit worst those that need most help. Means testing, says the report, is administratively costly, can discourage saving and reduces incentives to work. Britain comes well out of the report in providing support for carers – most European states do not bother – but it notes that Britain actually spends less on welfare than any of the other big European states, about 27 per cent of GDP in Britain compared to 31 per cent in Germany and France.

Politicians may be wrong in assuming that the electorate will not accept the realities of securing a reformed system of welfare. We all have an interest in ensuring that those out of work or the needy and sick are properly cared for. In a changing economic climate where the growth in job insecurity is a major feature the wealthy middle classes can now expect to be recipients of benefits, other than the general payments such as child benefit, at some time in their careers. It is surely in everyone's interest that those benefits are properly targeted and aimed not merely at alleviating the symptoms of joblessness but also at encouraging and helping people back into productive work.

Conservatives

During the last Parliament the Conservatives have been faced with the full implications of the current benefits system sapping public funds. As a party they are pledged to a substantial reduction in public spending with the aim of passing the savings back to the population in the form of lower taxes. The benefits system stands in the way of this objective. Yet at the same time the Conservatives have not felt able to advocate root and branch reform of the system; their efforts have in general been deployed to tinkering in the hope of reducing the overall bill. Thus benefits have been reorganised and cut back to stiffen entitlement and reduce the number of claimants. Much of this process has laid the party open to criticism. In 1995 it announced that it would be introducing orders into Parliament to cut the eligibility of refugees waiting for the outcome of appeals against Home Office decisions to deny them political asylum. The savings were modest by government standards but the policy produced the bizarre sight of a Conservative council, Westminster, taking the Government to Court on the grounds that they would be forced to pick up the cost of providing for these refugees.

There are now signs that the Government, with a general election looming, is engaging in the process of developing a new strategy for benefits. Major has made repeated calls in his recent speeches for a 'ruthless' reappraisal of spending and an energetic search for savings in public spending. He regards the reduction of dependency on the Welfare State as one of the main priorities of 'the next phase of Conservatism'. The signs are of a process that aims at more than a mere trimming of the budget, although there will be no retreat from a public position that the

Conservatives will continue to fund education and the NHS from taxation. Conservative sources have instead talked of a change in culture, a process of persuading people to provide for themselves through private insurance against the tragedies of sickness or unemployment and against the costs of their retirement, and of a development that aims welfare spending on getting people back into work.

One of the major and controversial targets for the Conservatives in recent years has been lone mothers, with policy proposals to cut their benefits floated at each Budget. The right have portrayed many single mothers as irresponsible parents, having children to boost their entitlement under the rules to a home and then sponging from the state for the rest of their lives. The figures do not bear this out. The vast majority of lone mothers are the victims of broken relationships, they are the separated or the divorced, forced to scrimp by the loss of one income and often unable, because of the cost of child care, to find work that will take them out of benefit dependency.

If proposals that seek to attack the benefits received by one-parent families emerge in the manifesto, it will be worth bearing some of the following facts in mind. At present 2.3 million or 20 per cent of children live in Britain's 1.4 million one-parent families. Of these families 58 per cent have problems paying for sufficient heating, a third of them lack hot water and 40 per cent of them live on under £100 a week. Only 2 per cent of two-parent families have to cope with such a low income. Those charities and pressure groups that represent lone parents point out that reducing their benefits and income will not help restore relationships or force mothers who already are unable to afford child care back into work. However, the manifesto may also detail policies designed to get single parents back into work with a series of pilot schemes giving assistance with child care costs when job hunting.

The other side of the Conservative equation on social security is the elimination of fraud. Benefit fraud costs the taxpayer some £1.5 billion each year. A recent crackdown on social security fraud netted the Government £654 million. Social security minister Peter Lilley has made a Conservative crackdown on fraud a central plank of his appeal to the country; at the 1995 Conservative conference he earned himself a standing ovation by offering £10 to each postal office worker who spots and reports a fraudster and by undertaking to introduce a benefits 'swipe' card, which would act as a benefit claiman's identity card and would help cut back on fraud. He called the card the claimant's 'inflexible friend'. The Conservatives will also try to change the law to enable computer cross-checking of benefit and tax records. A new 'fraud inspectorate' will be established to keep an eye on local authorities who are thought to be less than keen on curbing illegal claims. Critics of the campaign against fraud claim that using the same resources to tackle underpayment of tax would net bigger savings, with a clampdown on tax evasion being up to fourteen times more profitable than a campaign against benefits fraud.

Clamping down on fraud, more private provision and a restriction of benefits to those who really need them are likely to be the centrepieces of any manifesto pledge. The detail of any new policy is only likely to become apparent after a Conservative win at the election, but the signs are still mixed. Peter Lilley is often thought of as an unreconstructed right-winger, yet even he has pursued a strategy of trimming back entitlement through small and steady changes to reduce the welfare budget while heading off any opposition. Any substantial reform will require far more thought and effort than appears likely or possible in the few months which the Conservatives have left before a general election.

Labour

Labour itself has had problems with social security policy. In 1992 the then Labour leader John Smith established a semi-independent Social Justice Commission, chaired by Sir Gordon Borrie, intended to seek views wider than those inside the party and to review the party's social policy. The Commission produced a lengthy report shortly after Tony Blair was elected as leader. The most noteworthy recommendation was that Labour should tax child benefit; the party did not immediately commit itself to such a policy although the idea was trawled to assess public reaction in a series of speeches and interviews. Instead Labour insiders derided the report as 'good on analysis but poor on proposals'. Blair himself appears to agree with that verdict and is reported to believe that Borrie's approach was too cautious. In November 1995 he detailed Labour's shadow social security spokesman, Chris Smith, to come up with radical proposals for an overhaul of the Welfare State in time for a general election. Smith, himself a Labour moderniser, assembled a team of experts to help him and established regular seminars to discuss a range of options. The emphasis was to work closely with other shadow departments to devise a co-ordinated strategy for the family which Blair wants reflected in any social welfare decisions. The aim was to provide Labour with a comprehensive blueprint for reform in six months. By the summer of 1996 a policy was not yet in place although the Party had rejected calls for increasing pensions in line with the rise in earnings. At the same time a proposal to cut child benefit for sixteen- to eighteen-year-olds and transfer the resources to training sixteen- to eighteen-year-olds from poor families has caused problems with those who defend the universal nature of the benefit.

Among the ideas considered by Smith and his team is an ambitious plan to integrate the tax and benefits system. This was rejected by the Social Justice Commission but has long been advocated by the Liberal Democrats. Taxing child benefit raises a mouth-watering £300 million but is controversial and will provoke opposition within the party. Smith is understood to prefer targeting the benefit to avoid the administrative problems of applying tax. The problems of providing for the elderly will be tackled with a review of pension provisions and help for those in nursing homes. Other proposals that will be assessed include a minimum citizen's income, another Liberal Democrat idea, housing benefit reforms and welfare-to-work schemes for lone parents.

The shape of Labour reforms to the social security system will be impossible to judge before Smith's team's report is in the public domain. In the meantime some of the pledges already made by Labour spokesmen give an indication on the way Labour thinking is going. Blair has already made lone parents a priority, inspired by an Australian scheme, the Jobs, Education and Training Programme (JET), where single mothers are given free child care and advice on education and training; Blair hopes to introduce a similar scheme in Britain. Start-up costs would be funded by Labour's proposed windfall tax and lone parents would be encouraged to work with the employment service to work out a career development plan. There would be a change in current benefits rules to remove the disincentive on lone parents earning more than £15 a week. Similarly, Blair has talked of providing a minimum guaranteed pension but also taking into account private and occupational provision in reforms of the state pension. The aim of a guaranteed minimum pension would be to take 1.5 million pensioners out of means tested benefit. All this would be part of a strategy aimed at removing unemployment traps that discourage claimants from seeking work and would be aimed at tying in with Gordon Brown's proposals for training and employing those under twenty-five.

There have been criticisms that Labour's few announcements on benefits and obsession with working groups hide a poverty of thought and policy on the Welfare State. A series of academic seminars, so the critics claim, creates an illusion of activity but in the end cannot hide the problems that all parties face on welfare reform. There is no big idea or quick fix solution to these problems or Gordon Borrie and his team would have found one. To expect Chris Smith to produce a comprehensive blueprint in six months and with no net cost to a future Labour government might be thought to be a triumph of hope over experience.

Liberal Democrats

The Liberal Democrats and the Liberal Party before them have been committed to merging the tax and benefit systems since the 1970s. This was previously treated with a certain amount of ridicule by the other parties, but it has often been the function of the third party to develop radical ideas which are then taken up by one or both of the major parties. So it is with a merged tax–benefit system. Labour's review team under Chris Smith is now giving it serious consideration. The purpose of merging the two is that the system becomes more easily understandable and simpler for the government to administer. Both objectives, if achieved, would be great advances. The numbers of benefits and regulations needed to apply them are a bureaucrat's nightmare and anyone who has been obliged to complete a tax return will be aware of the complexities of the taxation system.

Under this system, for each benefit entitlement a person has they would instead receive a tax credit. If those tax credits exceed their tax liability than the state would pay them. If, on the other hand, their tax liability exceeds their credits then they would pay the state. Many of the anomalies of the current system would simply disappear. There is a popular fiction that National Insurance contributions go into a government pot from which our unemployment benefit and pensions are paid. In fact successive governments have treated the contributions as revenue and spent them as soon as they were received. The Liberal Democrats would end the pretence by merging National Insurance into income tax. Such a reform removes the need for employers to maintain contributions records and would simplify employers' contributions to their employees' welfare. To cover the state pension a portion of income tax would be earmarked for that purpose. By abolishing the contributory system the Liberal Democrats also assert that entitlement would change. The amount of benefit received would no longer hinge on the contributions paid but would related to need.

The Liberal Democrats agree with the other parties that the current benefits system traps people in unemployment and poverty. They share the objective of creating a springboard from which people can go into work and independence. In detail the Liberal Democrats claim that they would be able to restore full benefit entitlement for eighteen- to twenty-five-year-olds, and an income support credit for sixteen- to eighteen-year-olds. There would be an additional credit, assessed on need to top up the basic state pension. The party would restore the maternity grant and death grant, both allowed to wither in recent years, and a new simplified credit would be introduced to replace Family Credit and Income Support. Child benefit would be increased by £5 per child per week, and this would be funded by getting rid of the married couple's extra income tax allowance, which the Liberal Democrats argue gives the same benefit to couples where both are working and enjoying two salaries as to those where only one partner is working. This proposal would cause some dispute with the Churches. The married couple's allowance is about the last thing left which provides any state incentive to marry and make a public commitment rather than cohabit.

For the unemployed the party is opposed to the current job-seeker's allowance. Instead it would set up a benefit transfer scheme where an unemployed person's benefits can be transferred to an employer for up to two years so long as the employer provides training. The creation of tax credits would also help to reduce the poverty trap. On housing benefit the Liberal Democrats would reform the system to ease the current tapers which, when taken together with other benefits, can lead to high marginal rates of taxation. They would provide loans for people to pay deposits on tenancies and introduce a new mortgage benefit, funded from the abolition of mortgage interest tax relief, to provide 100 per cent assistance for home owners on low incomes.

All of these policies are more or less laudable and there is no doubting the Liberal Democrats' commitment to providing a civilised and smoother-running benefits system; however, strong doubts have been expressed within the party on whether or not some of the more ambitious elements of the policy are really affordable. Such a radical reform of the Welfare State would be far from easy and those seeking a fairer system would be well advised not to hold their breath while they wait for a Liberal Democrat government to implement their promises.

A note on housing

The aim of providing a home for everyone is one shared by every party, but over the last two decades homelessness has become an endemic problem in Britain. Under recent Conservative governments there has been an emphasis on promoting home ownership through the sale of council houses; this policy was severely damaged by the housing crash of the late 1980s, leaving many tenants-turned-buyers with worthless properties. The sale of homes and the growth of housing association provision have also reduced the role of local authorities in providing public housing, and there is now an estimated shortage of at least 100,000 homes in the rented sector. For the owner-occupiers the prospect of making quick profits in domestic property dried up with the fall in house prices, to be replaced by the twin problems of negative equity for an estimated 1.5 million households with mortgage debt higher than the value of their homes, and repossession, with lenders taking back up to a thousand homes every week. Meanwhile there has also been a growth in homelessness: 170,000 households became homeless in 1994, there are more than a million households on local authority waiting lists and there has been a decline in the quality of housing stock, with up to 1.6 million homes declared unfit to live in, although most of them are still occupied. The roofless poor sleep and beg in the doorways of our major cities, and families and benefit claimants are housed in temporary, shabby, hostel and bed and breakfast accommodation. The plight of this latter group brought considerable criticism for the government, which produced a Homelessness Review to co-ordinate policy to tackle the problem. In the summer of 1995 the Government published a new housing White Paper, *Our Future Homes*, which amounted to the most significant review of housing in politics for a decade and has concentrated policy debate on all areas of the subject.

Conservatives

In the White Paper the Conservatives maintained their commitment to encouraging private ownership and housing provision, aiming to provide a further 1.5 million people with the opportunity to own their own homes. This is set to continue the trend by which housing spending by government has more than halved since 1979. They aimed to increase the amount of social housing available to those who could not become owner-occupiers and to improve their living conditions by curbing anti-social behaviour on council estates. There was also the objective of ensuring that no one needs to sleep rough. The Conservatives are concerned that people are making themselves homeless to jump the queue to social housing, also maintaining that local authority housing is often going to non-priority cases. To tackle these problems they propose a reduced duty on councils only to provide temporary accommodation for those who have no alternative to sleeping rough. This proposal has drawn considerable criticism from the Churches and housing pressure groups. Councils will have a further duty to provide adequate housing advice services. The rent guarantee scheme is to be extended, as is the rough sleepers' initiative in London, which will be considered for other cities.

On social housing, the Conservatives are committed to improving and extending the housing available by attracting private finance into the sector. Commercial providers will be allowed to compete for grants with housing associations, there will be further transfers of council housing to the private sector, new Housing Investment Trusts are designed to attract the financial institutions into the market and Local Housing Companies will combine public and private sectors to become the main providers of social housing. Red tape is to be cut back to allow empty properties, currently running at 864,000 nationwide, to be used for short-term tenancies and for helping owners regain control of property when tenants have defaulted on their agreements; this includes the introduction of a probationary period in tenancies to ensure that tenants will not behave anti-socially. There will be regulation of landlord profits to ensure that there is no return to Rachmanism but there is still argument over how much, with the Treasury pressing for a hands-off approach. Housing benefit will be capped, a proposal opposed not only by the lobby groups but also by the Government's own Social Security Advisory Committee. The right to buy is to be extended to housing association tenants, with a new fund established to help them finance their purchases. The knife is out to cut government spending on housing by reducing support for mortgagees on benefit and by making housing renovation grants discretionary rather than mandatory. The Conservatives hope that these measures will provide a further 180,000 homes by 1998.

Labour

The Labour Party plans to launch a full-scale housing policy in March 1996. It has been delayed twice, having been due for publication in the summer of 1995 and in January 1996. Critics claim that the party lacks a housing policy, but the truth may be more that the Labour leadership is treading cautiously because of a dispute within the party over the role of Local Housing Companies. Many Labour local authorities see this as privatisation by the back door, and have proposed quasi-autonomous companies under the control of councils. The leadership is, however, keen to involve the private sector if only to cut the government's spending on housing. A future Labour government would not seek to increase spending except by releasing funds raised from the sale of council houses. Current indications are that the leadership will resist pressure from the grass roots to give councils a majority share in Local Housing Companies; instead there will be a series of safeguards, including contracts between the companies and local authorities and covenants over the transfer of housing stock. There will be guaranteed council representation on the boards of the new companies with blocking rights to stop them becoming PLCs. The companies would also be responsible to the Housing Corporation, which currently supervises housing associations. On housing improvement grants Labour has abandoned a scheme to set up improvement loans in favour of one to introduce smaller loans, available over a broader range of property rather than targeted at areas with special problems.

Liberal Democrats
The Liberal Democrats' policy on housing is set out in their Federal Policy Paper *A Place to Live*. On homelessness, they place great emphasis on reviewing tenancy rules to make more tenancies available to the homeless and support them in getting on the housing ladder with loans and higher benefits, some of which, such as extending housing benefit to sixteen- and seventeen-year-olds come with the proviso 'if resources allow'. They also plan to give councils draconian powers to use any property left empty without good cause to house homeless people, including making available 11,000 empty homes owned by central government.

For tenants, they aim to encourage private investment by increasing incentives for landlords but linking them to improved standards. Tenants are to be given new rights over the management of their homes, including new tenant management schemes. The party would separate the financial and monitoring functions of the Housing Corporation by transferring responsibility for allocating funds to councils, and they would give tenants and councillors a right to be represented on housing association committees.

For home owners, the party is pledged to extend shared ownership schemes and mortgage-to-rent schemes targeted particularly at people with mortgage arrears. They would introduce a new mortgage benefit for homeowners, concentrating government assistance on those who need it most and paying for it by phasing out mortgage interest tax relief.

Summary

It would appear from the numbers in difficulties with mortgages that the current level of home ownership is unsustainable. Against this background the Conservatives have been criticised for seeking to extend private ownership; this, claim the critics, will merely aggravate the current position. Encouraging private investment in housing must be a good thing although no one can predict whether the Conservatives' proposals will have this effect. There must be some concern that housing associations will be competing with private companies for government grants and this may have the effect of forcing up rents to fund the competition. I have been unable to find any commentator who approves of the Conservatives' policy for the homeless or believes that it will improve provision for the most vulnerable members of our communities.

Judgment must be suspended on Labour's housing policy until it is published. It must be regrettable that in the interim the party is being plagued by a largely ideological dispute about private or public provision. A more trenchant criticism of the proposals on the table rather than a desire to protect Labour local authority power would have been more reassuring.

The Liberal Democrats have some interesting ideas but some notable vote-losers. Virtually everyone agrees that mortgage interest tax relief, a subsidy to the middle classes which artificially increases house prices, should be phased out or abolished, but only the Liberal Democrats are brave enough to say so. The powers to house the homeless by requisitioning empty properties would also have a major impact on the market and cause major ructions with the voters. Perhaps the major criticism of Liberal Democrat policy is that it does not have the attraction of private finance as a centrepiece. As in other areas of policy-making, all the parties are hampered by the lack of available funds to improve housing.

Education

Britain's educational system has been consistently used as a political football over recent decades and there are two reasons for this. The voters care about our schools and universities and parents know that their children's future is heavily dependent on achievement at school; as a nation we care about education. Second, education is the subject of a heated ideological debate where the right wing's emphasis on choice confronts the left's insistence on equality. There is much that joins the parties on education but this is the rock that destroys consensus. No one can disagree with equality of opportunity, no one can disagree with parental involvement, but many in Labour find it difficult to see beyond their crusade for the destruction of class advantage, in which state education is a crucial weapon. The different sides of the debate are pursuing apparently irreconcilable goals and this explains much of the passion and froth generated in debate.

Our education system also feeds into the state of our society. Pick any political problem from crime and family breakdown to industrial competitiveness and health policy and those who present the arguments will sooner or later offer better education as a solution. Crime could be cured by teaching children to respect others, failing companies can be revitalised by highly skilled teenagers, computer-literate since primary school, and the general economy will benefit as well. Education is the nation's investment for its future and a crucial determinant in allowing any person to achieve their full potential.

A major element of the debate is a discussion on how standards can be improved in schools, and this ranges from the importance of nursery education through class sizes and homework regulation to the standards we set both teachers and pupils. There is no doubt that many schools are under serious pressure, with teachers overloaded with bureaucracy and pupils huddled into over-large and under-resourced classes in decaying buildings. In 1995 Duncan Graham, the man responsible for the early development of the National Curriculum, commented that it was designed for classes of twenty-five and said that he would doubt that a class of over thirty-five pupils would be getting value for money under the system. A notorious leaked memo from Education Secretary Gillian Shepherd revealed her fears that education was threatened by under-investment and lack of resources.

One of the remarkable differences between education policy and any other area of policy is the detail into which politicians of all parties are prepared to go in setting out their stalls. Labour is prepared to say precisely how much homework a primary-school pupil should be set, while the Conservatives will delve publicly into the mechanism for increasing the number of schools in the grant-maintained sector.

Education policy is also about political power and control. Spending on education is the third massive commitment of the Welfare State, and local authorities have had a central part to play in dispensing the money and calling the shots on local education policy. The emphasis over the last sixteen years has left that local authority involvement dented but still strong; they have lost their control of the curriculum, they have lost their ability to fund and decide policy for some schools in their areas, but they are still the major player in the vast majority of the nation's state schools. A major part of the debate concerns whether or not their involvement is a help or a hindrance to the pursuit of a better educational system.

Education is also about money. The newly merged Department of Education and Employment, merged to highlight and improve the link between schooling and careers, is one of the biggest spending departments. Both major parties enter the election debate pledged to financial and fiscal responsibility; if their spokesmen are to be believed, public borrowing will not rise whichever party wins power. The debate centres on how the system can be improved for a minimum cost, for additional resources for education will mean smaller spending in other causes. Only the Liberal Democrats are committed to increasing taxes to fund their policy. The rival party spokesmen are therefore forced back on reorganisation with no ambitious plans that cannot be obviously financed by economies elsewhere.

Perhaps because of these constraints, many of the policy initiatives echo each other, and there are frequent accusations of policy stealing. I suspect that this does not cut much ice with the voters; they are less concerned with the dogma of education policy and more concerned with how to get their children into the school of their choice to receive the best education possible.

One area of expansion in recent years has been higher education; this has been closely linked on the one hand to the need for skilled and educated graduates for the nation's workforce, and on the other to ensuring that with dire employment prospects as many young people as possible remain in the education system. Full-time students do not receive the range of benefits that would be available to them if they were out of college and out of a job. At present two out of every three young people will have some experience of higher education, but the dramatic increase in places and competition for students is also working itself out in problems for the higher education sector. There are accusations that the quality of students and graduates is dropping, that gaps are opening between a new English Ivy League of Oxbridge and top universities and a larger pool of routine institutions whose graduates have less hope in a tight employment situation.

The race is on again to find the means for a further expansion in higher education, if only to compete with our international competitors, but finding the means is not easy in a system that provides full state subsidy for fees and a part subsidy for maintenance. Novel ways of making students and their parents carry more of the cost of higher education, particularly in the form of loans or vouchers, are being considered by all parties. The result has been an increase in student poverty as the maintenance element of the grant has been frozen, with loans repayable after graduation supplied to fill the gap. Attracting private finance for this has been difficult. Many graduates can never afford to pay back the loans. An estimated £142 million may never be repaid.

All the parties are committed to providing a system of education that serves our children well and produces the skilled and educated workforce that Britain needs, but another element has entered the debate as the parties race towards the polls. There is a new readiness to discuss the importance of moral values in education and the need for the system to bolster and reinforce shared norms to produce model citizens. This used to be highly unfashionable, and there is still a devotion to value-free education in the teaching unions. This may have had its day. Since John Patten began the fight-back on values during his time as Education Secretary the emphasis has changed. Tony Blair himself now emphasises a fourth 'R' to add to the three that every child should learn: the fourth 'R' stands for Responsibility

Conservatives

The Conservatives have put education policy at the centre of their appeal to the electorate for a further term in office. In a series of speeches John Major has talked of a 'contract between the generations'; he has described education as a high priority for funding, exempt from the 'ruthless' determination to prune down public spending and expenditure on the Welfare State in particular, and has pledged his support for ensuring that every child receives the best education possible. But there have been problems in the Conservative camp, with Education Secretary Gillian Shepherd warning that education is suffering from under-resourcing, and in that leaked memo pointing out that there could be a voter backlash against the Government on its plans for higher education, with 'sudden detrimental changes to higher education alienating middle-class youngsters and putting at risk both their votes and the votes of their parents'. She goes on to recommend that the Government spends less time talking about the mechanisms of education and instead emphasises words that people find attractive, 'such as standards, discipline and choice'.

At the heart of Conservative policies to increase choice and excellence is a concentration on raising standards and liberating schools from what the Conservatives see as the dead hand of local authority control. The Conservatives have trumpeted a plan to boost nursery education with a voucher scheme, offering the equivalent of £1,100 for each four-year-old child to be used to purchase nursery education in either the private or the public sector. A pilot scheme was launched in the autumn of 1995, but the Government was disappointed by the lack of local authority co-operation. The amount per child was only sufficient to cover half the cost of a nursery place and was unsupported by extra resources for teachers and capital expenditure. Labour criticised the policy as a failure to honour a previous Major pledge to provide a nursery place for every four-year-old, though the Conservatives have countered by saying that no target date had been set for implementing the undertaking.

The Conservatives have always been seen as champions of the independent sector. The assisted places scheme, which pays towards the fees of 33,000 children whose parents could not afford independent schooling, was introduced by the Conservatives in the cause of expanding parental choice and giving greater opportunities to those who could not afford the education offered at private schools. For the next election Major has promised that the Conservatives will double the number of places. The scheme currently costs £110 million and would be abolished by Labour.

But the cornerstone of Conservative policy on secondary education is encouraging schools to opt out from local authority control. This, the party claims, frees schools from the restrictions imposed by councils on their spending and in particular allows them to select pupils. There is some survey support for the beneficial effects of opting out. A report compiled by Brunel University in 1995 claims that opted-out grant-maintained schools provide substantially better teaching and tighter dis- cipline than schools under council control. The survey showed 70 per cent of responding schools had increased spending on the curriculum, 87 per cent spent more on new books and new teaching methods, 86 per cent more on equipment and 90 per cent more on staff training. But persuading schools to take advantage of the opportunity for achieving grant-maintained status has not been easy. So far just over 1,000 of 25,000 schools have opted out. At the current rate it will take a century for all schools to be grant maintained and the Conservatives are casting round for ways to encourage the process. Among these could be measures to reduce the democratic element in the opting-out process. At present it is necessary to ballot the parents; the decision could be left to the governors alone. Alternatively, all local authority governors could be replaced by elected parent-governors or the more revolutionary move could be taken of transferring the budget for schools in its entirety from local authorities to a central school-funding agency. The latter option is bound to cause some flak for the Government, particularly as schools' spending is now local authorities' largest spending commitment, but it has the virtue of achieving grant-maintained status for every school at a stroke.

The Conservatives are also keen to introduce proposals for upping standards in schools. Gillian Shepherd is herself on record as being committed to abolishing 'communication by grunt' among adolescents. At the pre-school level, parents will receive progress reports on their four-year-olds and goals will be set for children in nursery. In secondary schools, problem pupils could be isolated in 'sin bins' for remedial teaching, although the Government has said that this initiative may be too costly; instead, head teachers could be given expanded and statutory powers to exclude the worst cases. The number of school children excluded from school has trebled in the last three years. GCSE English will in future contain a separate mark for a pupil's facility in using oral English and the broadcaster Trevor McDonald has been given charge of a new £250,000 unit to lead a campaign for better English. Head teachers will have a new professional qualification in a drive to improve standards and parents will be included by being required to sign contracts, pledging support for school rules and homework, to secure the place for their child. Many schools currently require a similar declaration.

A plan on the drawing-board to lower the school-leaving age to fourteen for those who do not benefit from academic classes and instead to cater for these pupils with practical on-the-job training has drawn considerable fire on the Government, with accusations of promoting child wage-slavery. However, this may be only a presentational problem. When a similar policy, described as bolstering student–workplace links with pupils seconded to employers to learn the skills required to get a job on leaving school, was trawled, it was more warmly welcomed. Government experts insist that pupils without academic aptitude become bored and disruptive when forced to study academic subjects but can be reformed by a dose of the real world, which shows them the purpose of their education and engages their interest in practical skills.

The Conservatives are also considering a major shake-up of higher education by offering vouchers to all pupils from the age of sixteen to be exchanged for education at the college or university of their choice. The vouchers would replace local authority grants but unlike grants, which cover total fees, they would cover only a minimum cost. Pupils with higher grades might obtain higher value vouchers, but students facing a shortfall would be required to meet it themselves or to take out a student loan. Repayment of these loans could be made easier than at present. Part of the attraction of this scheme is that it will reduce the costs of higher education, but it has come under fire for favouring the wealthy, who would be able to afford any extra outlay involved.

Labour
With the advent of New Labour there has been a revolution in Labour educational thinking, with a willingness to consider all options. This has fuelled considerable argument within the party, with the left alleging that the old aims of comprehensive education have been abandoned and highlighting each case of Labour front-bench spokesmen sending their own children to selective or grant-maintained schools. The process of rethinking policy is far from complete and a variety of ideas is being tested on both the party and the country. However, the final shape of Labour education policy is forming and for many critics it appears surprisingly similar to many of the Conservatives' policy proposals.

On nursery education, Blair is said to have accepted the plan to introduce vouchers if the Government can achieve a nationwide launch in the months preceding a spring election, but the party is considering proposals to trump the Tories by offering higher value vouchers. It is thought electorally impossible to enter an election pledged to remove the vouchers which have just been issued; instead the party would offer vouchers covering the full cost of a place for four-year-olds and a part-time place for three-year-olds. Labour local authorities remain opposed to vouchers, on principle as a right-wing dogma and on the detail that they would remove resources from council nursery schools by transferring public funds to private nurseries. Labour concurs with the Government on the need to inspect nursery schools but wants local authority representation on inspection teams, which would be required to report bad teachers to the head teacher. Labour would also want primary-school children to learn a foreign language.

Opting out has caused considerable fuss within the Labour Party, with rumours that the party would back selection. Stephen Pollard, the research director of the Fabian Society, a Labour think-tank, has advocated the dropping of all Labour shibboleths on education and encouraged the party to embrace wholeheartedly opting out, selection and vouchers. Meanwhile David Blunkett, the Labour front-bench spokesman, has ruled out selection, and the party has been desperately searching for a compromise on those schools that have already opted out. A modified form of grant-maintained school, floated at the last Labour Party conference, was attacked by Roy Hattersley as an abandonment of the comprehensive principle. Instead the party has been emphasising its commitment to better school discipline and smaller class sizes. On the latter Labour has pledged to reduce all classes to a maximum of thirty pupils in classes for five-, six- and seven-year-olds within the first year of a Labour government. They have costed this pledge at £60 million and have said that it will be paid for by abolishing assisted places. However, Labour is not entirely opposed to diverting public funds to private schools, for in a separate announcement David Blunkett has declared his readiness to consider subsidising children with a special artistic or musical talent in independent schools offering particularly good education in these areas.

On discipline and the detail of schooling Labour has announced a number of proposals. Every child would receive an education development plan with targets for improvements, and schools will be expected to set their own development plan, again with targets for improvement. Schools that conspicuously fail their pupils will be closed if there are alternative places nearby, or reopened under a new head teacher, with a new name and new governors. The staff would have to reapply for their jobs. The party is reviewing the A level system, and considering introducing a broader-band qualification which would not have such a high drop-out rate. Labour joins the Conservatives in recommending a new qualification for head teachers, but is also committed to introducing a new grade of super-teacher with more qualifications and skills. In an attempt to improve the quality of teachers, inspectors will be required to write unpublished reports on those that do not make the grade. There will also be guidelines for homework, with primary-school pupils expected to do a minimum of half an hour a night and secondary-school pupils a minimum of one and a half hours every evening. Parents of disruptive children could be given Parental Supervision Orders by the courts to attend special classes run by the Probation Service on bringing up children. Another idea under consideration is the issuing of identity cards to all schoolchildren to cut truancy; the police would be able to demand to see the card which would have to be endorsed by a teacher if the pupil was permitted to be away from school. Much of this has been derided by the left as yet more examples of Blair's lurch to the right.

Labour is also shadowing the Tories on their proposals for putting fourteen year olds out to work with local employers. David Blunkett has been monitoring a scheme at Glaisdale School in Nottingham, where all fourteen- to fifteen-year-olds are offered courses including practical placements leading to National Vocational Qualifications. Blunkett is said to have commented that the scheme was 'an excellent way to teach skills, without dividing children into sheep and goats'. But Labour's plans for secondary schools have run into considerable opposition from the teaching unions. There have been warnings that teachers are becoming the 'whipping boys' of education, blamed for every shortfall on expectations as the parties vie for the title of the toughest on standards in schools, while Nigel de Gruchy of the National Association of Schoolmasters/Union of Women Teachers said that there is not 'a snowball's chance in hell of these proposals being delivered without significant additional expenditure'.

Further promises in the manifesto may include measures to boost Internet use in schools, encourage state school links with Oxbridge, create safer travel routes to schools and boost literacy. On the Internet, Blair has pledge a private-public partnership to reduce link-up costs for schools with the franchise for providing a specialised educational network put out to tender. Other spokesmen have advocated 20 mph speed limits outside schools and special summer school literacy classes for those who fall behind in reading and writing.

On higher education, Labour's plans are expansionary. It wants more opportunities in further and higher education which it sees as part of a 'seamless robe' of life-long education. Part of this would be delivered by a new University of Industry which would cover work- and home-based learning and encourage part-time education. On the funding of higher education Labour has retreated from the principle that it should be free. Now it is advocating 'learning accounts' funded by contributions from students, employers and the state and held by a National Learning Bank. This would begin by supporting adult and part-time education but would ultimately be expanded to full-time provision. The current loans scheme would be scrapped, but payments would be rescheduled over a longer time and as a percentage of earnings. Fees would be paid through learning entitlements, which the party insists are not vouchers.

Liberal Democrats

The Liberal Democrats are remarkable for being the only party in the education debate to identify the main problem as underfunding and volunteering the information that they would add a penny to income tax, if necessary, to put an extra

£1 billion into schools. This sort of pledge is normally regarded as electoral suicide, but in this case it has been widely welcomed as an example of political honesty which the rest of the system would do well to emulate. The Liberal Democrats themselves regard it as a vote-winner. In general their education policy follows along the same lines as the other parties. They are committed to providing nursery education for every three- or four-year-old whose parents want it. They want to set each education department the target of a maximum class size of thirty in primary schools. They are not as disturbed as Labour by the implications of selection or opting out, indeed they favour the maximum freedom for schools within what they call a 'light touch' framework of local authority supervision. They justify this by pointing out that schools are a community resource and the council the representatives of the wider community, and they continue this line of thought by urging more community use of school facilities.

They join the other parties by advocating parent–school contracts and have a policy on tackling bullying, but there is far less emphasis on getting tough on disciplinary standards – indeed, there is rather more effort put into devising policies for encouraging healthy school meals and giving children a training in good nutritional habits. For those at fourteen plus they recommend an English baccalaureate to replace A levels, which would imitate the French system of academic and practical modules within a student's course; this could include work placements for sixteen- to eighteen-year-olds. They would extend an entitlement to education, either full- or part-time, through to nineteen-year-olds.

For teachers, the Liberal Democrats would introduce a new General Teaching Council as a professional body with the job of improving standards and dealing with poor teaching. They propose a programme of support for teachers struggling with the job, and incentives such as sabbaticals and secondments to keep good teachers. The Liberal Democrats also depart from the pack in giving a high profile to the role of IT in education.

On higher education, the Liberal Democrats are committed to expansion but there is still party debate on how this will be funded. The party is planning for two million students by the year 2000, restoring benefits entitlements and scrapping the student loans scheme. They would like to put comprehensive maintenance support in place for all full- and part-time students. The price tag for this is £7.6 billion. While the public might bear a penny on income tax, the prospect of upping that by another 4p is distinctly unwelcome and therefore the party is considering a range of measures to raise the money. Many of the initiatives are similar to Labour's. Students and employers could be asked to contribute to the cost through a central 'learning bank'. The party reckons that the cost of this will be so high that students might have to be asked to contribute to their own fees after the second year.

Summary

There is likely to be a considerable consensus on education when the manifestos are published. In fact we are likely to see an undignified rush to outbid each other among the parties in the run-up to an election. Extra nursery places are promised by all parties, with the Tories and Labour opting for a voucher system; the difference here is that the Labour scheme would go wider than the Conservative by funding the full cost of a place and offering part-time provision for three-year-olds.

The major difference on secondary schools, at least in rhetoric, is over selection and opting out. But in reality it will be difficult for Labour to dramatically change the status of the 1,000 grant-maintained schools. A more likely outcome, if Labour gains power, will be a combination of independence with some local authority representation, perhaps on the Liberal Democrat 'light touch' model. Much of the parties' recommendations on discipline and standards is not new and is already good practice in the best schools. It is up to the individual voter to judge how much of this is 'hot air' and an attempt to seem tougher than the other side. There is a real difference between the Conservatives and Labour over the assisted places scheme. Labour's proposal to fund artistically gifted children from low income families on places in private schools will not replace the scheme and there is nothing to say whether Labour will honour the current

Government's pledges to the education of the 33,000 children already benefiting from an assisted place.

Higher education has the greatest unanimity. All the parties' education think-tanks want to see expansion, all of them want to see the costs shared among state, employers and students. Vouchers for higher education are a dirty word in left-wing circles, but substitute the phrase 'learning entitlement' and Labour and Liberal Democrat policies look similar to the Conservative proposals.

There is more emphasis among all the parties on the need for values and responsibilities to inform standards in education once more. This has yet to reach beyond the stage of vaguely approving comments, but if there is really going to be an improvement in the education we offer our children it must surely take centre stage. Whether any political party will give an unqualified statement of support for this, and back it up with the policies to introduce values back into the system, remains to be seen.

Devolution

Those who venture north of the border, or west into Wales, become aware that they are visiting different countries. It's not only the fact that in both places there are different languages in everyday use but also that there is a different cultural environment, with the addition in Scotland of a separate national Church and legal and education systems. Both, however, are governed as part of the Union that forms the United Kingdom and that Union has formed a running sore in British politics for at least half a century.

The Scottish Parliament voted itself out of existence and for Union in 1707, amid allegations of mass corruption and English bribery. The Welsh became part of the United Kingdom as a conquered nation. Politicians from both countries have been agitating for some form of special recognition, or for changes in any existing recognition, since modern democracy came into being. The Liberal Democrats and their ancestors the old Liberal Party have been committed to devolution since before the last war. In 1969 the Conservative Prime Minister Edward Heath commissioned Lord Home to produce plans for a Scottish assembly. Labour have been divided on the issue; in 1979, under Liberal pressure in the Lib–Lab pact, they held a referendum on devolution in Scotland. The majority of votes cast opted for devolution, but a group of Labour MPs, some of them Scots, had managed to hedge the referendum about with rules that meant that at the end of the day the vote was officially lost. Both Wales and Scotland have their own nationalist parties pursuing the goal of full independence from England. For them devolution is merely a step on the longer road to national freedom.

Devolution is on the political agenda again and this general election may be the point at which a government is elected with a policy to introduce both Welsh and Scottish assemblies. Whoever wins the election, it is likely that there will be a substantial increase in the special recognition awarded to both Scottish and Welsh MPs. In part this is because of the Conservatives' continuing unpopularity in both Scotland and Wales. In Wales they have been unable for some time to find a Welsh Conservative MP capable of taking the job of Secretary of State for Wales. The post has instead been filled by a succession of English MPs. In Scotland the party has plumbed the depths of electoral unpopularity, standing at a derisory 13 per cent in the latest opinion polls and managing to hold on to 16 out of 72 constituencies by some of the smallest majorities in Britain. Opinion polls record that 70 per cent of Scots favour some form of devolution, but it is not at the top of their list of political priorities; when rating issues by their political importance Scottish voters rank employment, health and education ahead of constitutional change. With the additional spur of opposition collaboration on devolution, the Conservatives are now minded to respond to electoral pressure.

For the Opposition has co-operated. In Scotland for the last six years a Constitutional Convention, ably chaired by a Presbyterian clergyman, Canon Kenyon Wright, has brought both Labour and Liberal Democrats together with representatives of Scottish industry, Church and society. They have produced a blueprint for an assembly with devolved powers which will form the basis of both Labour and Liberal Democrat manifestos at the next election. The Scottish Nationalists, with their demand for full independence, have boycotted the Convention.

The details of the Convention's proposals are explained further under Labour and Liberal Democrat policies. In general, the assembly would consist of 129 members with powers to legislate on a broad range of Scottish policy and with a power to vary the general tax rate by 3p. This has given rise to two areas of political debate: the so-called 'Tartan Tax' and the 'West Lothian question'.

The Tartan Tax

According to Conservative critics a Scottish Parliament would add £6 a week in tax to every Scottish household and jeopardise £5 billion worth of investment in Scotland's economy. There has been some concern expressed by Scottish industry, which, while sympathetic to devolution, tends to oppose a Scots Parliament with tax-raising powers. They suspect that this would lead to higher taxes and inevitably damage inward investment and industry's ability to attract employees from outside Scotland. This criticism is worth taking seriously. In practice the power to vary income tax should never lead to lower taxes. Scotland is a net recipient of funds from the UK government, accounting for 10 per cent of public spending compared to its 8.8 per cent of the UK population. It is unlikely that English MPs would continue to vote for this level of Scottish grants if a Scots Parliament was giving its own people lower taxes than the rest of the UK. Equally, English MPs might question the need to provide generous grants if Scotland was raising more in taxes than the other nations in the UK.

Scotland does suffer from a weak financial position. In 1993/4, Scotland raised £20.4 billion in taxation, excluding the benefits of North Sea oil, but spent £28.4 billion. These totals suggest that on the same spending pattern, Scotland would have a 15 per cent deficit of GDP, excluding oil, compared to 8.5 per cent for the UK in general. It would be a brave politician who could expect to lop 15 per cent off Scottish spending and balance the books that way. The normal reply to this is that Scotland should enjoy the benefits of oil revenue and that that would make up the difference, but unfortunately this is no longer practicable, even assuming that the UK Parliament was prepared to hand all of the oil revenue over to Scotland. Government receipts from oil taxation amounted to just £1.2 billion in 1993/4 and £1.6 billion in 1994/5, still leaving a large deficit.

The West Lothian question

The origin of the term is unclear, although it was first used by Enoch Powell in 1977 and may be named after Tam Dalyell, the old-Etonian Scots laird who sits as Labour MP for Linlithgow but was MP for West Lothian in the 1970s. He is a trenchant critic of devolution. The current form of the question is as follows: 'Why should Scottish MPs representing Scotland in the UK Parliament be allowed to vote on English domestic matters if English MPs are not allowed to vote in a Scottish Parliament on Scottish domestic matters; and what are the implications of this problem for Scottish representation at Westminster after an assembly has been set up?'

At present the people of Scotland could be said to be over-represented in Parliament, with more MPs per head of the population than most regions in England. If the number of seats was distributed on a pro-rata basis Scotland would get only 59 compared to 72 at present. Should Scots' representation be cut after an assembly comes into being, and if so to what level? A cut in Scottish representation would strike an immediate blow to the Labour Party, which elects a high proportion of Westminster MPs north of the border. To the opponents of devolution the beauty of the West Lothian question is that it cannot be answered. Those who support devolution contend that it's irrelevant, or fall back on proposals for English regional devolution to balance the equation.

Conservatives

The Opposition has, over the last sixteen years, accused the Conservatives of treating Scotland as a conquered fiefdom. Due to the Westminster system the Conservatives have formed the government for Scotland with not only a minority of the popular vote but also a minority of MPs. There have been accusations that Scotland has suffered as a result, with the country being used for experiments in the wilder Thatcherite policies of the 1980s. Scotland, for example, had the poll tax first, in what was alleged to be a dry run for the rest of the country. Throughout this period the Conservatives have been resolutely opposed to proposals for a devolved assembly, but there has been movement in the last year. It now appears that the Conservatives are trying to undercut the Opposition by granting devolved powers to other institutions in the Scottish government to draw the teeth of the devolution tiger. The new proposed powers affect three bodies, the Scottish Grand Committee, the new unitary authorities and the Scottish Economic Council.

The Scottish Grand Committee comprises all Scottish MPs and has the role of discussing Scottish affairs. It occasionally meets in Edinburgh, in the hall set aside for any future assembly. The Committee has been something of a talking shop, and has been rather cavalierly treated in the past. For a substantial period in the early 1990s the Committee did not meet at all. Now the Government proposes a greatly expanded role. Michael Forsyth, Scotland's Secretary of State, has said that in future Bills affecting Scotland could come before the Committee for second and third readings 'whenever it makes sense to do so' and take evidence from outsiders at the Committee stage of Bills. The Committee will also play a role in questioning ministers on policy matters affecting Scotland. The Conservatives have proposed a similar system for the Welsh Grand Committee, except that the Welsh MPs will not be given the same legislative role as the Scots. The Government justifies this by reference to Scotland's separate legal and educational systems. The opposition parties have been highly critical of these proposals, deriding the Grand Committees as mere talking shops. Significantly, the Government will decide which legislation goes before the Scottish Committee, and opponents allege that the Conservatives will limit this to uncontroversial measures.

Another plank of the Conservative proposals to undermine devolution is increased powers for Scottish local authorities. They will have a greater say in decisions on allocating money from their grants to transport, education and social work. Planning applications for fewer than ten houses will no longer have to go before the Secretary of State and specific grants for teacher and social work training will be abolished. There may be further powers announced on regulating drinking in public places. Many of these powers had been requested by the Convention of Scottish Local Authorities (COSLA) and the Government's announcement of them was welcomed, but COSLA also pointed out that the capping of local government spending would continue.

Finally, Michael Forsyth is planning to take advice from the Scottish Economic Council, a group of businessmen and union leaders who will deliberate on the Government's spending plans more openly than they do at present.

Labour and Liberal Democrat

The Labour and Liberal Democrat proposals on devolution come jointly from their work on the Convention. Under them, and in the first year of a government led by either party, a new Scottish Parliament of 129 MPs would be established. Of these, seventy-three would be elected from the current constituencies on the first-past-the-post system and a further fifty-six from eight new regional constituencies on a proportional system. An MP would not be allowed the 'dual mandate' of a seat in both Westminster and Edinburgh. The Parliament, which would consist of a single chamber, would meet for a four-year fixed term; MPs would elect a Chief Minister from their number, and they would have the power to debate domestic issues such as education, training, health, local government, industrial affairs and home and legal affairs. They would also have the power to raise or reduce tax by up to 3p in the pound. Under a common agreement, each party would try to ensure that at least half of its candidates in winnable constituencies were women.

In the summer of 1996 a rift appeared between the Liberal Democrats and Labour as the latter lost their nerve on devolution. In a matter of months, Labour policy shifted from no referendum to one referendum with two questions, to two referendums and then back to one referendum with two questions. In an attempt to halt the derision this caused in Scotland, Labour claimed that they would use a referendum to confer a popular mandate for the introduction of legislation for a Scottish Assembly within the first year of a Labour government.

John Major has branded the idea of a new Scottish Parliament as 'loony' but his is hardly a measured criticism. Both parties still have questions to answer on the Tartan Tax and the West Lothian question, but more definition can be expected as the parties finalise their general election programmes.

The Nationalists

The Nationalists want full independence, but point to their desire for full membership of the European Union and close ties with the United Kingdom; they would promote the creation of an Association of States of the British Isles. They would wish to establish a single-chamber Parliament with full legislative powers. It would consist of 200 MPs elected by a PR system with two-thirds from the existing parliamentary constituencies and a further fifty-six elected from party lists. There would be an elected Chancellor as the presiding officer, but the Queen would remain the Head of State. Scottish peers would have to seek election to the new chamber. The Nationalists would want Scotland to be a full member of the Commonwealth, the UN and NATO, but they want a non-nuclear Scotland and would therefore withdraw from the command structure. They would introduce a new Bill of Rights, which would include rights to housing, health and education, and this would be included in a written constitution. The Parliament would give the Gaelic language official status.

Many of these proposals are shared by the Welsh Nationalist Party, Plaid Cymru. However, in Wales the Welsh language already has official status. Plaid Cymru has welcomed Liberal and Labour support for a Welsh Parliament but warned that the price for Plaid support for the proposals depends on the new assembly being elected by proportional representation and having teeth.

Summary

After years of supporters campaigning for some degree of devolution in both Scotland and Wales, there is now a real hope for some progress, no matter which party wins the election. The Conservatives have to a certain extent found themselves caught between the devil and the deep blue sea on this issue. For years they have ignored the recorded wishes of the people of both nations for more devolution. They now find themselves in the position of either being portrayed as admitting that there was indeed a legitimate grievance or being seen to come to the debate with too little, too late. Michael Forsyth's proposals for local government and the Scottish local authorities are an ingenious attempt to square the circle. It remains to be seen whether or not it will convince Scottish voters that this is a real devolution of power or whether they will feel that the Conservatives are in fact advocating a chimera of increased powers while keeping the real power firmly in London with its satellite Secretaries of State.

Labour and the Liberal Democrats are to be commended for having co-operated so constructively on the Convention, but the battle for an assembly is far from over. There remains a significant element in the Labour Party committed to fighting devolution every step of the way, and a Blair government with a small majority and in the face of a back-bench revolt might have to solicit support from minority parties to fulfil its pledges. The Liberal Democrats are of course also committed to English regional assemblies. Blair has flirted with this idea but it is unlikely to reach a Labour manifesto. The nationalists may consider themselves in the perfect position to win whatever happens. Should a government fail to introduce devolution, they can expect recruits and support from disillusioned voters and they probably believe, even though they did not participate in the Convention, that it is a small step from a devolved to an independent Scotland.

This issue has further ramifications. National assemblies elected on a proportional basis will bring PR to the British mainland for the first time. For those who see the reform of the electoral system as a crucial precondition for more general reform this could be a significant chink in the armour of first-past-the-post. Once PR is here it could well become the preferred system to be used whenever a section of our democracy receives a dose of constitutional reform. It is not impossible to picture a reformed House of Lords with a proportionally elected element leading to PR for the European elections and eventually PR for the Commons itself. Under this scenario the establishment of Scottish and Welsh assemblies could be the first step in a programme of constitutional reform that would outstrip the Great Reform Act of 1832 in its scope and effect on British politics.

The moral agenda – life issues

Morality is becoming a fashionable term in Parliament again. Tony Blair's saying that 'Labour is a moral crusade, or it is nothing' was greeted with rapturous applause. It was not always so. In the 1960s, 1970s and 1980s, if you used the word 'moral' you were branding yourself as a reactionary, preaching outmoded values irrelevant and distasteful to the modern world. Now the term is on the lips of politicians again and they are using it because of an increasing realisation, bolstered by the activity of groups espousing Judaeo-Christian values, that society will not work as an amoral struggle by individuals for primacy and can only work as a co-operative venture where mutual responsibilities are recognised.

This is the stuff of political philosophy and it is not easy to translate it into political practice. The stresses and strains of the economy and established systems frustrate the best intentions. Our political parties between them carry considerable ideological baggage, and the dogmas of radical socialism or right-wing Thatcherism are alive and well on the benches of the Commons. It has been said that in a political system such as ours the extremes of right and left will dominate the centre between elections, even though the party which captures the moderate ground is more likely to win the election. This has certainly been true of British politics in the past. It is difficult to imagine Blair saying much of the New Labour message in the Labour Party of 1983; indeed, in 1983 Blair, now a committed European, found it necessary to underline his support for withdrawing from the European Community. John Major is currently something of a prisoner of his own right and many of his speeches seem constructed to mollify his own right wing. If Labour wins the next election there is a real possibility that Blair will be held to ransom by the Old Labour forces, keeping their own counsel now for fear of a row that could cost them victory at the polls, but unlikely to be so unrestrained if Labour forms a government. Many commentators have noted that this is the reason for the warmth between Labour and the Liberal Democrats. Blair may need their votes if he is to keep his own left wing in check.

In one sense all of politics is a moral question. The amount we give to the starving in the world, the tax cuts or the tax rises we give to the fat cats of our own industry, whether or not we pursue a green farming policy, all involve moral judgments as much as whether or not we allow abortion. For this reason I have always been uncomfortable with the notion of the 'conscience vote', the decision by a party to allow a free vote on issues of moral controversy. All votes should be conscience votes, and the notion of an MP voting against their conscience because they are whipped by the party organisers is repugnant to most people in the country. In fact the conscience vote is a device to avoid embroiling political parties in what they would see as a no-win situation. On many 'conscience' issues the views on either side are particularly strongly held. Political tacticians tend to retreat or temporise in the face of conviction because they know that by coming down on one side they will alienate the other. Allow room for conscience and the problem disappears; the party can sit happily on the fence and avoid antagonising both the public and its own members who happen to hold trenchant views on the issue under discussion.

This chapter is an opportunity to consider particular issues which do not sit happily under the party political framework. There is great public interest on these subjects and they invariably come up at questions at general election meetings. Most candidates will have their answers off pat but it is worth pursuing them. We can learn a great deal about the mettle of the men and women competing for our votes if we can discover the values that motivate them.

The issues here may seem arbitrarily chosen. I could have written at length about animal rights. The Conservatives, with some notable exceptions such as Anne Widdecombe, are generally in favour and talk of the freedom of choice to pursue field sports. Labour has an anti-hunting policy, but intriguingly has no problem with blood sports such as fishing. The Liberal Democrats are also opposed to hunting but a significant number of their MPs choose to defy the party line. It would be cynical in the extreme to speculate on the reasons for this and explain it away as a class-based reaction. Hunt supporters are more generally Conservative; fishermen, especially anglers, are more generally Labour voters.

There are other issues such as pornography, gay rights, smoking, divorce, television violence, drugs and family issues which I could have covered at length if space allowed. On family issues I would argue that virtually every area of policy outside the conscience vote has an impact on families. It is now more common than it was for politicians to claim that they are champions of the family. As with many other areas of policy, the proof of the pudding is in the eating. The Movement for Christian Democracy has advocated the introduction of family impact statements for all legislation with a social impact. Legislation is already subject to environmental statements to discover its impact on the environment, and we have business cost compliance statements where civil servants have to spell out the likely impact of legislation on the finances of British business; the one area that is not covered is the family. Until we place the family at the heart of the policy process we will not reverse the frightening statistics of family breakdown with all the poverty and misery that that causes.

One common feature of all 'moral' issues is that they pit one person's rights against another's. That is symptomatic of our age, for we have become obsessed with rights. Our society claims rights in every area of our lives and the primary right is the right to choose whatever we want. Such choices have become valueless for it would be an infringement of rights to question the value or morality of another person's choice. This baleful influence of an over-emphasis on rights has eclipsed notions of duties and responsibilities. We all owe these to others and to society at large; one of the challenges facing us is how to balance rights and responsibilities and on what principles we base such a balance.

There is a final reason why these issues should be at the forefront of our minds when we consider how we will vote. I write this with Labour as the favourite to win the election. A new Labour government will inherit a stagnating economy and a massive national debt. It will be pledged in its manifesto to be financially and fiscally responsible. It will be committed to cutting taxes for the majority of the population and the net effect will be that it will not have the resources to tackle many of the problems that it will face or to fulfil many of the more optimistic promises it has made. A government in this position will be tempted to turn to measures which grab headlines and keep the activists happy but do not carry a substantial cost. In Labour's case these will almost certainly be both constitutional and moral. On the latter, legislation extending the Abortion Act to Northern Ireland, on voluntary euthanasia and gay rights would all fit the bill. It is even possible that it will take the route of Labour governments in the 1960s, which allowed measures on such subjects to go through in the name of back-bench MPs as Private Member's Bills, but provided government time to get them through, as well as Civil Service help with drafting and parliamentary procedure. All these issues are not only topics for today but form the controversies of tomorrow.

Abortion

Life issues go to the heart of a person's political beliefs, for they confront, at a basic level, how we regard the human being who is after all the subject of politics. It is again the question of rights, pitting those who believe in the right of every human being to life against those who seek to balance other rights against that life. To debate the issue from the basis of rights provides two separate lines of argument. Those who are in favour of abortion and the woman's right to choose argue that during pregnancy the rights of the mother are dominant over any right of the child to life. They see rights as developing over the first period of life; many would argue that the baby only possesses a right to life that exceeds the mother's right to choose when it is capable of breathing, at about twenty-four weeks' gestation, others maintain that the point of birth is more appropriate and still others would not grant a baby or infant a right to life until it is capable of existing without the support and care of other humans.

For those who take a pro-life position the right to life can never be equated with size or development. Life is an absolute right because without it no other right can be enjoyed, and it extends to all members of the species. The pro-life movement would argue that all of us depend on others to survive, whether we are in or out of the womb. Finally they would argue for a balance of rights between mother and child. Both mother and child have a right to our care and support and that can never involve taking the life of either mother or child, except in those rare circumstances when because of medical complications the life of the child threatens the life of the mother.

Such a right to life is not recognised in British law. The law itself is ambiguous and bears the marks of the ferocity of the debate on this subject. Abortion, or 'causing a miscarriage' is still an offence under British law punishable by up to life imprisonment. But since 1967 and the Steel Abortion Act, it has been a defence against the charge to say that the abortion was carried out under the grounds mentioned in the Act and certified 'in good faith' by two doctors. The extent to which the Abortion Act applied was limited by another Act, the Infant Life Preservation Act, a piece of Victorian legislation aimed at the practice of killing a baby during the course of birth, which specified that for the purposes of the law a baby was considered capable of being born alive at twenty-eight weeks' gestation. In 1991 this was uncoupled from the Abortion Act, allowing abortions after twenty-eight weeks and right up to and including birth. As a result, since 1991 the numbers of abortions over twenty-eight weeks have more than doubled.

The Abortion Act was introduced with the promise that it would make every child a wanted child, and was proffered as the solution to homelessness and child abuse. It was argued that it would only be invoked in the most serious cases and was sold to Parliament liberally illustrated with stories of hard cases. Nearly thirty years afterwards, more than three million abortions have been carried out, with under 10 per cent of them being for reasons of disability or serious danger to the mother's life or health. Over 90 per cent are carried out on 'social' grounds, and of those more than 90 per cent that mention a medical ground are done under the guise of a 'neurotic disorder' or a 'depressive disorder not elsewhere classified'. More than half of all abortions are now done in private clinics, many of which have financial links to referral agencies. To this extent instead of the limited access to abortion which Parliament intended, we now have abortion on demand in this country, in that it is virtually impossible not to find doctors who will issue a certificate.

Abortion, and the medical procedures associated with it, is now one of the most common operations for obstetric and gynaecological departments and doctors. The 1967 Act guaranteed freedom of conscience for those doctors who refused to take part in abortion. That protection does not extend in the same way to nurses, and there was also no mention of chemists or hospital workers. The conscience clause was a sop to opponents of the legislation and a means of reassuring those who wavered on the Bill. As the workload of abortions piled up, so hospital departments became increasingly reluctant to appoint doctors who refused to participate in the work. As a result those who hold a pro-life view of uncompromising care for both mother and child have been progressively squeezed out of obstetrics and gynaecology. Chemists and hospital porters were not so fortunate, and there have been recent cases of a chemist being sacked for refusing to prescribe the abortifacient drug RU486, and hospital porters disciplined for refusing to burn the bodies of aborted babies with the hospital waste.

The proponents of abortion rights are still not satisfied with the law as it stands. Many would wish to see it extended, and there are various campaigns that may raise their heads again in the next Parliament. In particular, the Abortion Act did not apply to Northern Ireland, and the pro-choice pressure groups have launched a campaign to persuade the Government to extend the law to the province. The main reason for not applying the Act in Northern Ireland is that the population is resolutely opposed to its imposition. During the last Parliament every Northern Ireland MP, whether nationalist or unionist, opposed the move, and the press conference to launch the campaign was sponsored by English abortion activists. The current Government has blocked extension. The Labour Party is committed to it.

Pro-abortion activists have had most success within the Labour Party. The National Abortion Campaign receives a significant part of its funding from union donations. Labour has had a policy in favour of abortion rights for years and it has been rigidly imposed. MPs voting against abortion have been hounded by their whips and the party secretariat, and threatened with reselection in their own constituencies. The Labour Life Group, which campaigns against abortion, has the distinction of being the only group within the party, apart from the Militant Tendency, to be deregistered as a recognised group. It has been barred from party conferences and its fringe meetings picketed. During debates on the Human Embryology and Fertility Bill, Labour MPs moved an amendment to create a public 'blacklist' of doctors who had registered a conscientious objection to abortion. This was not a fringe amendment; one of its supporters was Tony Blair.

The Liberal Democrats have also flirted with abortion rights. A pro-abortion policy position passed by a recent party conference was only rescinded when David Alton MP threatened to stand down in protest at the next election. The party has since substituted a compromise formula which can be interpreted as pledging the extension of the Act to Northern Ireland. The Conservatives have been equally compromised. It has been Conservative ministers who have presided over the workings of the Act for the past sixteen years and they were the government in power when the abortion laws were relaxed further in 1991. On that occasion the party applied a whip to the third reading of the Bill, threatening ministers who voted against with dismissal from their posts. Many chose to be absent and record an abstention instead. In the same legislation doctors and scientists were given powers to experiment destructively on the human embryo. A Conservative government has also funded the international organisations working in the notorious one-child population control programme in China which includes forced sterilisation and abortion.

Much of the theory behind both abortion and the abuse of the human embryo is eugenic, the theory that the human race can be improved if the right people breed and the wrong babies are stopped from being born. Thus the Abortion Act discriminates against the disabled by allowing disabled babies' lives to be taken, up to and including the moment of birth. Much of the pressure from abortion legislation has come from groups which have their origin in the eugenics movement of the 1930s which affected much of the Western world besides Germany.

Marching hand in hand with abortion and experimentation on unborn human beings is euthanasia. During the last Parliament British courts took the first steps on the road to euthanasia by granting permission for patients in a persistent vegetative state to be deprived of food and water until they died. Parliament considered legislation in both Lords and Commons to legalise forms of euthanasia. The legislation was withdrawn in one case and not proceeded with in the other, but a Lords Committee on Medical Ethics considered the issue and overwhelmingly rejected the arguments for voluntary euthanasia. The Government is currently considering further legislative proposals from the Law Association which would open the door to forms of euthanasia. Surveys of MPs' views show an increase in support, although still a minority, for such legislation. But it will not stop there; more legislation and more pressure will be applied to Parliament in the future. All parties are currently neutral on the subject but this would not stop any of them, when in government, providing time for a Bill. The debate on these issues will if anything intensify, whoever wins the election.

Getting Involved

Getting involved

General elections benefit from as many people as possible being involved. In the last century politicians pulled the sort of crowds that would only be seen at football matches or pop concerts today. Gladstone could give an off-the-cuff speech standing on top of a carriage on an open hillside with an audience of thousands; no politician would consider doing such a thing today without a full public address system and extensive notes. But the remainders of our Victorian electoral system are still with us and they are there to be taken advantage of. Candidates want to meet as many people as possible; they want to be visible. Being a candidate is when a politician is most vulnerable – they are, after all, soliciting your vote. Traditions can vary from seat to seat. In many rural seats there is still pressure for a candidate to appear in every village or hold a meeting in every village; not to do so would risk the inhabitants assuming that they had been slighted and voting another way. Political meetings are less common in urban seats but even then most parties will attempt to hold two or three meetings during the course of a four-week campaign. Other local bodies may invite all the candidates to take part in a joint meeting and throw the event open to all. Local churches commonly perform this role. Finally there is always the media, with local newspapers reporting local candidates and some of them being exposed to the terrors of live phone-in programmes on local radio.

Lobbying the candidate

Using the system properly requires some sound research. If you want to beard your local candidates on an issue of your choice, and particularly if you want to persuade them to support a particular cause, it pays to have done your homework. Your local library will be able to help. The first question is: How important is the candidate you are meeting? All candidates are not of the same value. There is little point convincing the Natural Law Party candidate to support your view; he or she will never reach Parliament to put your case. Work out instead which candidate is the favourite to win and which candidate looks likely to be the challenger. These are your best targets. The best way to do this is to use a national political guide such as *Dod's Guide* or *The Times Guide to the House of Commons* to look up the results last time round. Unfortunately for this election there have been massive boundary changes in some seats; to assess these consult *The Almanac of British Politics*, which normally suggests a notional result based on local election figures in the wards that make up the constituency. Your local papers will also be a help. Most of them will run an assessment of the situation in your constituency during the opening stages of the campaign. Often the likely winner of the seat will be public knowledge. If you're in a rock-solid Labour inner-city safe seat you should not need even to visit your library.

Finding the candidate you want to meet can occasionally be difficult. You have a number of options. Many candidates hold advice sessions to take up the cases of the constituents they want to represent; these may be advertised locally or on the election literature that political campaigners stuff through your letter-box. Alternatively you can telephone the party offices listed at the back of this book; remember, many candidates are in place long before an election is called, particularly those with a real chance of winning. Failing these, the local offices of the party should be able to help and you can often get telephone numbers of local councillors from the various parties who should be able to put you in touch with their candidate from your local authority's offices.

Visiting the candidate is important. Time will be limited and it is crucial that you make the best use of yours. Before the meeting consider the case you are going to put. What are the main reasons in favour of your case and what are the main objections? If it helps make a list and then make sure that you can answer the main objections if the candidate makes them. If you have the time and resources, get together a brief statement of your case with any supporting material to present to the candidate when you meet. It will remind him of your meeting and get a second shot at him when – or if – he reads your papers.

When you meet the candidate make your case clearly. A candidate can lose interest as well as the thread in a long and rambling statement. Try and ensure that you have a variety of things that you want the candidate to do. Are you running a petition? Ask him to sign. Can he write to his party leader to support your cause, or would a letter to the local council be more appropriate? Asking him to do these things puts a candidate on the spot, and remember, he wants to charm you and win your vote: all the pressures are on him to agree to do something for you even if he cannot bring himself to say he wholly supports your case.

If you think that you have just visited your next MP make a point of writing to him to confirm the details of the meeting, particularly if he has agreed to do something for you or if he declared support for your cause. Having his reply confirming the details is useful ammunition if he is ever tempted to desert your cause in future. Consider telephoning your local press to tell them the results of your meeting.

The other forum for meeting a candidate is in the street or in a public meeting. The pressures on your quarry are different in each case. On the street the candidate's aim is to meet and shake hands with as many people as possible. His agent will have supplied him with a group of people to back him up and create the illusion of an active working team. He won't want to spend fifteen minutes chewing the cud with you. He could visit and meet up to thirty people during that time in any shopping street in the constituency. If he is tempted to spend a few minutes and his team is really professional they will try to move him on. They may even supplant him with a campaign member to take your details and mollify you while your quarry slips off to boost his image with the voters down the street. All the more important, then, for you to make an impression and ask direct and relevant questions. If necessary use the time to ask when you can meet him to discuss the subject at further length. You're unlikely to have your case prepared and your papers in order if you meet him on the street.

At the political meeting much depends on the chairman and the format for questions. At some church meetings you may be asked to submit your question in writing first with no guarantee it will be answered; make sure that you phrase it succinctly and neatly and, if you wish, ask for a supplementary question in case you want to come back at the candidate's answer. Don't be afraid of standing up and asking for that right, and pressing it, within reason, if the chairman is tempted to deny you the chance. A good chairman will want the meeting to appear open and tolerant, not stage-managed and closed. A practised chairman will rule you out of order in the hope of slapping you down early if he thinks he can intimidate you. If you insist, his next option is to present you as a troublemaker, for then the sympathy of the meeting will be with him rather than you. Cast yourself in the role of decent constituent merely asking for clarification with all the traditions of fair play and freedom of speech behind you. You will not want to alienate the audience either, so be prepared to back down graciously if it looks as though that may be happening. You might ask when the next opportunity will occur to follow up your question.

There may also be a chance of pressing your case after a meeting. This has the advantage of giving you a bit more time; you may even get an extended interview if there is no pressure on the candidate. Remember first to check his schedule, as many candidates may do two or even three public meetings each evening and if you are at the first they will dash out of the hall to speed away in a waiting car before you've had a chance to corner them.

Failing the chance of meeting the candidate, you can always write. The rules here are much the same. Keep your letter short and to the point and include any relevant material to support your case. Allow up to two weeks for a reply. Politicians are not the most punctual of correspondents and remember, the candidate may be trying to deal with a hundred letters such as yours.

Working for a candidate

You may be fortunate enough to find a candidate of whatever party who you think deserves to be elected. Do not hold back; every election campaign team needs workers. If you're committed enough to seeing this candidate elected make a point of volunteering your services. The first thing to realise is that you do not need to be a member of the party to help. While the bulk of campaign workers will be local party members no one is going to question your bona fides if you turn up and proffer your services. Do not expect to be included in the back-room strategy sessions at once; you will have to prove you're reliable and acquire some expertise first. Depending on the size of the campaign anything is possible. At one of my first by-elections I began by spending two days in a windowless cellar pasting posters to boards, and then found myself appointed candidate's driver for the rest of the campaign. In a hotly contested seat campaigns can number anything up to fifty workers. In a small campaign with little better than paper candidacy you will be able to count the number of workers on one hand.

Elections are exhausting, extremely hard work and great fun. If you work at it all week, all campaign, rather than at weekends or the odd evening, then expect to require a day off to recover. Campaigns have two main objectives, to get the message of the candidate across and to identify the candidate's vote and your opponents' vote. Getting the message across involves two main tasks, publicity, such as posters, and leafleting. Identifying the vote involves canvassing house to house. Both require basic organisation, which you can expect from the campaign team. As a beginner you may be required to do any of the mundane tasks associated with setting up for leafleting or canvassing. Election offices are not centres of high-tech excellence; letters still need to be addressed by hand or have labels stuck on them, leaflets still need to be counted out and packaged into road and street deliveries, canvass cards are now more usually run off a from a computerised electoral register but a fair number of constituencies will still operate on a scissors and glue basis, cutting up a copy of the electoral roll and pasting it on cards. Sooner or later you will be asked to leaflet or canvass; in areas where numbers are short you may be asked to do both at the same time. Leafleting can be a lonely and depressing job and it is good practice to send people out in teams. After delivering to a neighbourhood you will have promised yourself never to inflict a letter-box at the bottom of your front door on your postman and will have conquered any fear of dogs you may have had, besides learning the mechanisms of all the more usual designs of garden gate. Canvassing is more fun; you interview the voter and seek to obtain an indication of how they are going to vote. This is not an excuse for a lengthy chat. The object of the exercise is to get round as many voters as possible. Wily opponents of your candidate may try to detain you with lengthy and convoluted questions on party policy, always holding out the hint of a promise to vote for your candidate if you give the right answer. If you enjoy meeting and talking with the voters, can adopt a brisk style and fancy an afternoon walk, then canvassing is for you. As a canvasser you will be able to gauge a neighbourhood as the evidence builds up on your card, and you will have constituency casework thrown at you to refer to the candidate. You may be equipped with posters to dispense to supporters of your candidate as they identify themselves to you; it's remarkably satisfying to wander down a street you have canvassed and see the posters up that you're responsible for.

In an ideal world those running the campaign will be crunching the numbers from the canvass cards and building up a register of your vote for polling day. If you've worked through the campaign from beginning to end you'll begin to realise what tribal loyalty really means. As polling day approaches all campaigns begin to gather pace. There's always too much work and too few people to do it. It's an exceptional constituency that conducts a complete canvass as well as going back to all the people who were 'out' when you called the first time. The climax of the campaign is the eve of poll meeting. By then you'll have a good idea of the prospects for the following day.

Polling day itself is a mountain of work. Some parties, notably the Liberal Democrats, deliver a 'good morning' leaflet as a final plug to the voters. This will involve you creeping round the streets in the early hours of the morning attempting not to bang gates or wake the dogs. During the day itself there are numerous jobs including driving voters to the polls – the Conservatives are noted for the number of cars they can field on polling day – the process of 'knocking up', and manning a polling station by standing outside to collect the numbers from people's polling cards. The atmosphere at the polling stations is usually cordial; by tradition the representatives of the various parties, suitably decked out with badges and rosettes, share the numbers and are normally extremely polite to each other. The voters tend to show their card numbers only to the representative of the party they voted for. You will be exceptional if you don't get a twinge of satisfaction each time someone approaches you instead of the others.

Ideally someone from your campaign will be touring the polling stations collecting the lists of numbers of those who have voted. Back at the committee rooms for that ward, normally someone's front room, the numbers will be crossed off lists of voters to prepare for knocking up. This involves squads of people descending on a street to urge those who haven't voted to get out and cast a vote. As the day progresses this process becomes increasingly frantic. Voters have an annoying habit of coming home from work and stopping for supper before casting their vote with half an hour to spare before close of poll. You may have called at the house three times before they leave to vote, your adrenalin will be at record levels and you will be more than a little exhausted. You will briefly wonder how the voter concerned can appear so calm. If the campaign is working well you will be straining to get the maximum vote out. There's nothing more depressing than to lose by a small margin and think, 'If only we'd worked harder . . .'

When the polls close you have the chance to snatch an hour's respite. You will then have to go, exhausted as you are, to the constituency party. I have always found these events trying at the best of times. Your mind cannot disengage itself from the constituency count, and a party, given the state of physical tiredness you may be in, is the last place you want to be. If you're very honoured you will be admitted to the count as an official scrutineer assessing the boxes as they're opened, keeping an eye on the counting and a record of the votes cast. A good team of scrutineers can predict the result long before it's announced and warn the candidate, who if he's been well prepared will have a victory speech in one pocket and a speech for defeat in the other. The result is declared from midnight onwards. If you're at the party you will be watching the television coverage, if at the count you'll be cheering or drying your eyes depending on the outcome. Elections are undoubtedly emotionally draining and physically exhausting but they're the red meat of democracy and everyone should be involved, at least once.

The MCD election hotline

As the campaign gets under way there will be many initiatives to inform the voters of what their candidates believe. Some of these will be organised by the churches and you may well find such a church meeting where all candidates get an opportunity to speak and answer questions in your area. There will also be prayers for the election; MCD itself organises a day of prayer and fasting at election time with the proceeds saved from the fasting going to a charity.

MCD's major election initiative is the production of a questionnaire which goes to all candidates of the main three parties and the manning of a voter-information hotline. The first questionnaire was issued by MCD during the 1992 election. At the time it was the largest survey of candidate opinion done both before and during the election. Candidates were asked to complete a form questioning them on the positions they took on a range of issues from pro-life matters to housing, overseas aid, personal debt and the environment. The questionnaire produced a 25 per cent response rate, which is considered high. The results were tabulated at a central office and phone lines manned to pass the information on to voters calling in. MCD will be undertaking a similar exercise in the 1997 election. The questionnaire is likely to cover more issues and the hotline number will be more widely disseminated than was possible in 1992. Check the religious and general press for details or contact the MCD Membership Office:

13 Winwick Lane, Lowton,
Warrington
WA3 ILR,
Tel. (during office hours): 01942–671 581.

Useful contacts

The Movement for Christian Democracy
13, Winwick Lane
Lowton
Warrington
WA3 ILR
Tel.: 01942–671 581

Westminster and Whitehall

House of Commons
London
SWIA 0AA
Switchboard: 0171–219 3000

Public Information Office
(Holds masses of useful information and can tell you in which constituency you live)
Tel.: 0171–219 4272

House of Lords
London
SW1A 0PW
Switchboard: 0171–219 3000

House of Lords Information Office
Tel.: 0171–219 3107

Government ministries

Ministry of Agriculture Fisheries and Food
Whitehall Place
London
SW1A 2HH
Tel.: 0171–270 3000

Cabinet Office
Whitehall
London
SW1A 2AS
Tel.: 0171–270 3000

Ministry of Defence
Main Building
Whitehall
London
SW1A 2HB
Tel.: 0171–218 9000

Department of Education and Employment
Sanctuary Buildings
Great Smith Street
London
SW1P 3BT
Tel.: 0171–925 5000

Department of the Environment
2 Marsham Street
London
SW1P 3EB
Tel.: 0171–276 3000

Foreign and Commonwealth Office
King Charles Street
London
SW1A 2AH
Tel.: 0171–270 3000

Department of Health
Richmond House
79 Whitehall
London
SW1A 2NS
Tel.: 0171–210 3000

Home Office
50 Queen Anne's Gate
London
SW1H 9AT
Tel.: 0171–273 3000

Law Officers' Department
(Attorney General, Solicitor General, Lord Advocate and
Solicitor General for Scotland)
9 Buckingham Gate
London
SW1E 6JP
Tel.: 0171–828 7155

Lord Chancellor's Department
House of Lords
London
SW1A 0PW
Tel.: 0171–219 3000

Department of National Heritage
2–4 Cockspur Street
London
SW1Y 5DH
Tel.: 0171–211 6000

Northern Ireland Office
Whitehall
London
SW1A 2AZ
Tel.: 0171–210 3000

Scottish Office
Dover House
Whitehall
London
SW1A 2AU
Tel.: 0171–270 3000

Department of Social Security
Richmond House
79 Whitehall
London
SW1A 2NS
Tel.: 0171–210 3000

Board of Trade
1–19 Victoria Street
London
SW1H 0ET
Tel.: 0171–215 5000

Department of Transport
Great Minster House
76 Marsham Street
London
SW1P 4DR
Tel.: 0171–271 5000

Treasury
Parliament Street
London
SW1P 3AG
Tel.: 0171–270 5000

Welsh Office
Gwydyr House
Whitehall
London
SWIA 2ER
Tel.: 0171–270 3000

Political parties

The Conservative Party
Central Office
32 Smith Square
London
SW1P 3HH
Tel.: 0171–222 9000

The Labour Party
150 Walworth Road
London
SE17 1JT
Tel.: 0171–701 1234

The Liberal Democrats
4 Cowley Street
London
SW1P 3NB
Tel.: 0171–222 7999

The Green Party
1a Waterlow Road
London
N19 5NJ
Tel.: 0171–272 4474

The Scottish National Party
6 North Charlotte Street
Edinburgh
EH2 4JH
Tel.: 0131–226 3661

Plaid Cymru
51 Cathedral Road
Cardiff
CF1 9HD
Tel.: 01222–231 944

The Alliance Party Of Northern Ireland
88 University Street
Belfast
BT7 1HE
Tel.: 01232–324274

The Ulster Unionist Party
3 Glengall Street
Belfast
BT12 5AE
Tel.: 01232–324601

The Social Democratic and Labour Party
611c Lisburn Road
Belfast
BT9 7GT
Tel.: 01232–668100

The Ulster Democratic Unionist Party
286 Shankill Rd
Belfast
BT13 2BN
Tel.: 01232–247440

The Referendum Party
5 Galena Rd
Hammersmith
London
W6 0LT
Tel.: 0181–563 1155

The UK Independence Party
30 Regent Street
London
W1R 5PE
Tel.: 0171–434 4559

International organisations in the UK

The European Commission
8 Storey's Gate
London
SW1P 3AT
Tel.: 0171–973 1992

The European Parliament
2 Queen Anne's Gate
London
SW1H 9AA
Tel.: 0171–222 0411

NATO
Room 306
Empress State Building
London
SW6 1TR
Tel.: 0171–218 9000

The United Nations
18 Buckingham Gate
London
SW1E 6LB
Tel.: 0171–630 1981

Pressure groups and other organisations

Age Concern England
Astral House
1268 London Road
London
SW16 4ER
Tel.: 0181–679 6069

Amnesty International
1 Easton Street
London
WC1X 8DG
Tel.: 0171–413 5500

Friends of the Earth
26 Underwood Street
London
N1 7JQ
Tel.: 0171–490 1555

Greenpeace Ltd.
Canonbury Villas
London
N1 2PN
Tel.: 0171–354 5100

LIFE
Life House
la Newbold Terrace
Leamington Spa
Warwickshire
CV32 4EA
Tel.: 01926–421 587

NSPCC
67 Saffron Hill
London
EC1N 8RS
Tel.: 0171–242 1626

National Association of Citizens Advice Bureaux
Myddleton House
115 Pentonville Road
London
N1 9LZ
Tel.: 0171–833 2181

National Council for One Parent Families
255 Kentish Town Road
London
NW5 2LX
Tel.: 0171–267 1361

OXFAM
274 Banbury Road
Oxford
OX2 7DZ
Tel.: 01865–311311

SHAC
Kingsbourne House
229 High Holborn
London
WC1V 7DA
Tel.: 0171–404 7447

Shelter
88 Old Street
London
EC1V 9HU
Tel.: 0171–253 0202

SPUC
7 Tufton Street
London
SW1P 3QN
Tel.: 0171–222 5845

The media

The Press Association
85 Fleet Street
London
EC1P 1BE
Tel.: 0171–353 7440

Television and radio

BBC (HQ and national radio stations)
BBC Broadcasting House
Portland Place
London
W1A 1AA
Tel.: 0171–580 4468

BBC Television
Television Centre
Wood Lane
London
W12 7RJ
Tel.: 0181–743 8000

The Independent Television Commission
33 Foley Street
London
W1P 7LB
Tel.: 0171–255 3000

Channel 4
124 Horseferry Road
London
SW1P 2TX
Tel.: 0171–396 4444

Newspapers

Daily Express
245 Blackfriars Road
London
SE1 9UX
Tel.: 0171–928 8000

Daily Mail
2 Derry Street
London
W8 5TT
Tel.: 0171–938 6000

Daily Mirror
33 Holborn
London
EC1P 1DQ
Tel.: 0171–353 0246

Daily Telegraph
1 Canada Square
Canary Wharf
London
E14 5DT
Tel.: 0171–538 5000

Financial Times
1 Southwark Bridge
London
SE1 9HL
Tel.: 0171–873 3000

Guardian
119 Farringdon Road
London
EC1R 3ER
Tel.: 0171–278 2332

Independent
1 Canada Square
Canary Wharf
London
E14 5DL
Tel.: 0171–293 2000

The Times
1 Pennington Street
Wapping
London
E1 9XW
Tel.: 0171–782 5000

Independent on Sunday
1 Canada Square
Canary Wharf
London
E14 5DT
Tel.: 0171–293 2682

Observer
119 Farringdon Road
London
EC1R 3ER
Tel.: 0171–278 2332

Sunday Telegraph
1 Canada Square
Canary Wharf
London
E14 5DT
Tel.: 0171–538 5000

Sunday Times
1 Pennington Street
Wapping
London
E1 9XW
Tel.: 0171–782 5000

Christian press

Alpha
37 Elm Road
New Maldon
Surrey
KT3 3HB
Tel.: 0181–942 9761

Christianity
37 Elm Road
New Maldon
Surrey
KT3 3HB
Tel.: 0181–942 9761

Baptist Times
129 The Broadway
Didcot
Oxon
OX11 8XB
Tel.: 01235–512012

Catholic Herald
Lamb's Passage
Bunhill Row
London
EC1Y 8TQ
Tel.: 0171–588 3101

Catholic Times
St James Buildings
Oxford Street
Manchester
M1 6FP
Tel.: 0161–236 8856

New Christian Herald
96 Dominion Road
Worthing
West Sussex
BN14 8JP
Tel.: 01903–821 082

Church Times
33 Upper Street
London
N1 0PN
Tel.: 0171–359 4570

Church of England Newspaper
10 Little College Street
London
SW1P 3SH
Tel.: 0171–976 7760

Methodist Recorder
122 Golden Lane
London
EC1Y 0TL
Tel.: 0171–251 8414

Prophecy Today
The Park
Moggerhanger
Bedfordshire
MK44 3RW
Tel.: 01767–641001

Scottish Catholic Observer
19 Waterloo Street
Glasgow
G2 6BT
Tel.: 0141–221 4956

The Tablet
1 King Street Cloisters
Clifton Walk
London
W6 0QZ
Tel.: 0181–748 8484

Third Way
St Peter's
Sumner Road
Harrow
Middlesex
HA2 4BX
Tel.: 0181–423 8494

The Universe
St James's Buildings
Oxford Street
Manchester
M1 6FP
Tel.: 0161–236 8856

Woman Alive
96 Dominion Road
Worthing
West Sussex
BN14 8JP
Tel.: 01903–821 082

Christian organisations and pressure groups

Church of England Board for Social Responsibility
  (General Synod)
Great Smith Street
London
SW1P 3NZ
Tel.: 0171–222 9011

CARE
53 Romney Street
London
SW1P 3RF
Tel.: 0171–233 0455

Catholic Association for Racial Justice
Talma Rd
Brixton
London
SW2 1AS
Tel.: 0171–274 0024

Catholic Bishops' Conference for England and Wales
39 Eccleston Square
London
SW1V 1BX
Tel.: 0171–630 5166

Catholic Housing Aid Society
209 Old Marylebone Road
London
NW1 5QT
Tel.: 0171–723 7273

Catholic Institute for International Relations
Unit 3
Canonbury Yard
190a North Road
London
N1 7BJ
Tel.: 0171–354 0883

Christian Campaign for Nuclear Disarmament
Bramall Lane
Sheffield
S2 4QZ
Tel.: 0114–273 9047

Christian Ecology Link
20 Carlton Road
Harrogate
North Yorkshire
HG2 8DD
Tel.: 01423–871 616

The Christian Institute
Eslington Terrace
Jesmond
Newcastle upon Tyne
NE2 4RF
Tel.: 0191–281 5664

Christians for Social Justice
31 Prince of Wales Lane
Yardley Wood
Birmingham
B14 4LB
Tel.: 0121–430 8980

Church Action on Poverty
Central Buildings
Oldham Street
Manchester
M1 1JT
Tel.: 0161–236 9321

Church of Scotland Board of Social Responsibility
Charis House
47 Milton Road East
Edinburgh
EH15 2SR
Tel.: 0131–657 2000

Conservative Family Campaign
24 Mamora Road
London
SE22 0RX
Tel.: 0181–299 2567

The Evangelical Alliance
186 Kennington Park Road
London
SE11 4BT
Tel.: 0171–582 0228

The Jubilee Centre
3 Hooper Street
Cambridge
CB1 2NZ
Tel.: 01223–311596

Justice and Peace (Scotland)
15d Hill Street
Glasgow
G3 6RN
Tel.: 0141–333 0238

The Maranatha Community
102 Irlam Road
Flixton
Manchester
M41 6JT
Tel.: 0161–748 4858

National Liaison Committee of Diocesan Justice and Peace
Groups
38 Eccleston Square
London
SW1V 1BX
Tel.: 0171–834 5138

Order of Christian Unity
Christian Unity House
58 Hanover Gardens
London
SE11 5TN
Tel.: 0171–735 6210

Pax Christi
9 Henry Road
London
N4 2LH
Tel.: 0181–800 4612

Quaker Social Responsibility and Education
Friends House
Euston Road
London
NW1 2BJ
Tel.: 0171–387 3601

The Rutherford Institute
419 Richmond Road
Twickenham
Middlesex
TW1 2EX
Tel.: 0181–296 1908

The Shaftesbury Society
16 Kingston Road
London
SW19 1JZ
Tel.: 0181–542 5550

Traidcraft
Kingsway
Team Valley Trading Estate
Gateshead
Tyne and Wear
NE11 0NE
Tel.: 0191–491 0591